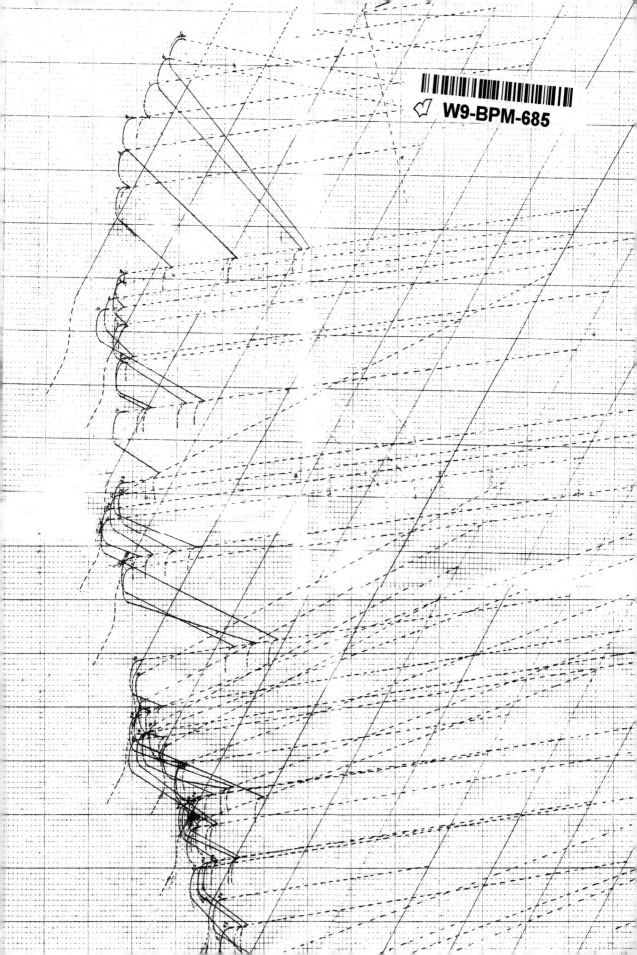

W9-BPM-685

September, 2004

David L. Hays
306090 07///// Guest Editor

Gerard Bul-lalayao
306090 07////Designer

Published by:
306090, Inc.
Emily Abruzzo
Alexander F. Briseño
Jonathan D. Solomon
Andrew Yang
Editors

Lynne DeSilva-Johnson
Assitant Editor

306090 Advisory Board
Paul Lewis
M. Christine Boyer
Michael Sorkin
Mario Gandelsonas
Christian Unverzagt
David L. Hays
Sarah Whiting
Mark Jarzombek

306090 is an independent architectural journal published and distributed semi-annually. 306090 seeks to publish diverse, inquisitive projects by students and young professionals that have not been published elsewhere.

Opinions expressed in 306090 are the author's alone and do not necessarily reflect those of the editors.

Distributed By:
Princeton Architectural Press
37 East Seventh Street
New York, NY 10003
1-800-722-657
www.papress.com

Contact publisher for Library of Congress Cataloging-in-Publication Data.

www.306090.org
info@306090.org

306090, Inc. is a non-profit institution registered in the states of New Jersey and New York. Your donations are tax deductible. For information on how to contribute or to submit work please contact us at: info@306090.org or visit our Website. For ordering information contact the Princeton Architectural Press at orders@papress.com.

06 05 04 03 6 5 4 3 2 First Edition
ISBN 1-56898-484-7
© Copyright 2004, 306090, Inc.

Cover design by Gerard Bul-lalayao. Photo by Chris Taylor. © 2002-2003, Land Arts of the American West.

Inside cover: Image by Elena Wiersma.

Pages 1, 208: Vector drawings by Kristin Schuster.

Page 3: Photograph by David L. Hays.

306090, Inc.
350 Canal Street
Box 2092
New York, NY 10013-0875

CONTENTS

306090

PREFACE \\\\\\ //////
PROSPECTS //////
POSITIONS //////
PROGRAMS //////
PROFILES ///
PROPOSALS \\\ //////

LANDSCAPE

The title of this volume, "Landscape within Architecture," refers in practical terms to landscape pedagogy within programs of architecture but also more abstractly to the sense that landscape has recently affected architecture from within. Until the mid-1990s, architects typically considered landscape architecture a discipline auxiliary to their own—an attitude reinforced by modernist isolation and ranking of the design professions.[1] Even worse, landscape was thought by some architects to be a dying discipline, sentimental in its preoccupation with nature and out of touch with the urban focus of contemporary life.[2] In truth, landscape architecture had undergone significant development since the late 1960s pertaining to ecological concerns and approaches (*e.g.*, large-scale hydrology, brownfield remediation),[3] but the relevance of that work to other areas of design had yet to be discerned. As recently as 1995, for example, Niall Kirkwood—already distinguished for his work in urban landscape—noted "[a] strongly held belief that the landscape architecture profession has been unable to contribute to a growing body of urban design exploration by architects, urban designers, and engineers."[4]

In the decade since Kirkwood's remark, attitudes about landscape have changed dramatically. In 1999, James Corner heralded "the apparent recovery of landscape, or its reappearance in the cultural sphere after years of relative neglect and indifference."[5] In January 2000, Paul Bennett called landscape architecture "a new frontier, a discipline perhaps more fertile for developing new concepts than architecture."[6] Landscape is now a leading theme in discourse on architecture and urbanism.[7] Although that interest is not entirely new,[8] the degree to which it has penetrated the core of architectural thinking is unprecedented.

Many have speculated about the reasons for the new preoccupation with landscape. For example, Bennett explained the turn succinctly as "context trumps objects," a formulation that also evokes the critical influence of design-school historians.[9] Corner has pointed to the influence of deindustrialization, postwar growth of recreation and tourism, and rising popular interest in ecology and the environment, among other factors.[10] Marc Treib has noted the appeal of regionalism, as a foil to globalization and homogenization, while underscoring time, "the crucial dimension of landscape," as a factor architects long to master.[11] Of course, more immediate economic and political factors have also been at play. Since the early 1990s, the profession of landscape architecture has become increasingly distinct and distinguished through independent licensure and a period of pronounced intellectual and economic prosperity. Landscape architecture has exceeded

WITHIN ARCHITECTURE (WITHIN LANDSCAPE)

architecture in unexpected ways, and many architects would like to engage with—if not to regain control over—that expanded domain of practice.[12]

Consistent among these arguments and observations is the idea that landscape is (now) within architecture because architecture is (always) within landscape. For much of the twentieth century, architects were trained to conceive and represent their work as if in isolation.[13] In keeping with the priorities of high modernism, context was acknowledged only in terms of formal and material aspects, primarily as apprehended through vision. When the structured illusions of modernism began to come undone, however, apprehensions about buildings as static and isolated objects quickly emerged in architectural theory and criticism. The qualities of stability and clarity long valued as attributes of monumentality became suspect because of their association with interpretive closure. In other words, the insufficiency of buildings as objects was attributed, in part, to their very pretense to the contrary. As shaping influences, rigid ideals of form, structure, and type were abandoned in favor of dynamic conditions, forces, and flows. "Performance" in architecture, long identified with resistance to formal and programmatic change, is now associated with responsiveness, flexibility, and adaptability, on the model of navigation. In theory and criticism, the ideal of resistance to

interpretation has given rise to an orthodoxy of inconclusiveness in which ambiguity, enigma, uncertainty, subtlety, and suppleness are highly prized.[14]

Landscape architecture, to which the instability now valued in architecture is fundamental,[15] suddenly appeared way ahead of the game. Landscape architects are trained to understand and work responsively with forces of change. Performance in landscape has always been a sort of navigation, in which expertise is played against uncertainty over time. The fact that architects have been turning to landscape for new methods and approaches is ultimately based on that condition.

During the past decade, a host of publications and events have addressed relations between architecture and landscape,[16] yet very little has been said about how programs of architecture are addressing the new interests.[17] That silence is ironic, given the central role of the academy in contemporary architectural culture, but it is perhaps explained, at least in part, by the real novelty of what is taking place. This issue of *306090* was conceived in January 2003 as an opportunity to contribute to recent developments by investigating, documenting, and interpreting the current state of landscape pedagogy within programs of architecture. The result is a cross-section of contemporary arguments and approaches selected for their diversity in addressing the common theme. The volume brings together twenty-five essays by thirty-one contributors—administrators, professors, and students—representing twenty-two public and private universities and institutes in the United States and Canada. The essays are grouped in five sections—prospects, positions, programs, profiles, and proposals—according to content and emphasis. Those categories are to be understood loosely, however, as most contributions pertain to more than one. The contributors were invited to illustrate their arguments with examples from their own experience. Consequently, the tone of the volume is both scholarly and personal. Some of the contributors address the idea of "landscape within architecture" directly, but others have transformed the title phrase to convey new meanings in keeping with their arguments—for example, "landscape into architecture" (Day), "architecture within landscape" (Hoversten), "architecture and landscape" (Ponte, Marpillero, Pollak), and "between architecture and landscape architecture" (Braham).

Collectively, the essays underscore four main lessons for architecture and landscape architecture alike. The first is that exposure to alternate theory and practice expands the way designers think both about and beyond aspects of work already familiar to them. The impact of architecture on landscape in that regard is one legacy of modernism and is now well recorded.[18] The reverse is the work of the present. For buildings to become more than objects, architects must recalibrate their field of perception spatially, temporally, and conceptually, moving beyond the limits of the building to the contexts in which their work will be situated and to which it will ultimately contribute. As part of that expanded thinking, architects—and architectural education—must address the environmental and resource-based challenges that have already begun to shape the future of the design professions. Landscape pedagogy and practice already offer useful models for how that might be accomplished.

A second lesson is to embrace time in practical as well as philosophical terms. In the chronology of the conventional studio project, a "research" phase is followed by a "design" phase leading ultimately to a "final" review in which a single scheme is presented as the best solution (i.e., the best the student could devise). That sequence stages design as a process of clarification, justification, and demonstration akin to a mathematical or scientific proof.[19] Yet, the process of design—like research in any field—is never as discretely formulaic as the typical narrative suggests, and the "final" scheme is never truly more than one instance extracted from a flux of shifting possibilities. An alternative approach is to treat the duration of the studio—not its "final" product—as the work to be evaluated. That focus on time as the substance of the studio acknowledges and underscores the fact that, in school as in practice, projects begin long before they are assigned, and they continue long past their ostensible completion through representation or construction.

A third lesson is to get students out of the studio. Just as architecture and landscape architecture are more than drawings, words, and ideas, the designer is more than a hand, a mouth, and a brain. Explorations of real space educate the body and mind in ways that cannot be achieved within the confines of the studio. For studio projects, remote sites known only through representations have great value in exercising the imagination, but sites that can be experienced in person over time introduce students to a host of qualities and concerns otherwise easily ignored. Local sites help students learn to "know their place." Projects are further enhanced when they engage people with real stakes in the issues being explored.

A fourth lesson for both architecture and landscape architecture is to move beyond appropriation by engaging in real collaboration. As Linda Pollak notes in this volume, "Acknowledging that they (don't) know different things can be a catalyst for students to collaborate across disciplines." According to Eliza Pennypacker, quoted here by James Wines, "one of the main benefits of creative interaction and outreach communication is that they eliminate misconceptions of other disciplines based on ignorance." In professional terms, the long-term implication of recent developments—whether we are witnessing the emergence of a synthetic type of professional or whether collaboration is ultimately a way of discerning specializations and thereby elaborating distinctions—remains unclear. The experiences and arguments presented in this volume suggest both possibilities. Yet, the question itself is perhaps not so significant, because it is clear, in any event, that synthetic approaches are now crucial and that the hierarchical division of design professions that characterized professional culture in the last century should be a thing of the past.

In keeping with that understanding, a specific objective of *306090 07* is to help break down boundaries between design programs within the same institution. Programs of architecture and landscape architecture are typically administered separately, even when housed in the same facility. That approach has deep roots and many sound practical justifications, but it is hardly absolute. The recent reorganization at the University of Virginia is a timely and much-discussed case-in-point, and high-level integration has long distinguished programs such as the Graduate School of Design at Harvard and the School of Architecture, Urban Design, and Landscape Architecture at City College of New York.[20] Furthermore, recent developments have brought architecture and landscape architecture together in ways that make pedagogical collaborations not only interesting but logical. The contents of this volume show how students, faculty, and administrators are crossing disciplinary boundaries to the benefit of architecture and landscape architecture alike.

Another objective of this volume is to foster communication between institutions. Many schools function in a surprising degree of isolation, even when geographically close to other programs with which productive exchange could be cultivated. Important landscape-related experiments are taking place in many programs, yet little information about them is being circulated beyond campus limits. For example, a large number of schools are undertaking new studio courses taught jointly by faculty of architecture and landscape architecture, with occasional participation from urban planning or design. Noteworthy examples—besides those described in this volume—include "Borderlands," at Auburn University; "Crosstown 116: Bringing Istanbul Home to Harlem," at City College of New York; a ten-week studio-abroad program in Portugal and Venice organized by University of Minnesota; and a new collaborative studio at the University of Michigan, to be taught annually by the Visiting Professor in Sustainable Design. The fact that so many programs are engaging in collaborative endeavors underscores the value of intercampus communication and the need for documentation and interpretation. *306090 07* is intended as a foray into that work and a catalyst for exchange between students, faculty, and administrators interested in understanding and expanding the presence of landscape within architecture.

David L. Hays holds an A.B. in Fine Arts and Romance Languages and Literatures from Harvard University, an M.Arch. from Princeton University, and a Ph.D. in History of Art from Yale University. He is currently an Assistant Professor in the Department of Landscape Architecture at the University of Illinois at Urbana-Champaign.

NOTES

1 _ See, for example, Marc Treib, "Nature Recalled," in *Recovering Landscape*, ed. James Corner (Princeton, NJ: Princeton Architectural Press, 1999), 29-43, and Paul Bennett, "The Other Side of the Fence: What Drives Landscape Architecture Now," *Architectural Record* (Jan. 2000): 58-62, 64, 194. For additional bibliography, see note 1 of the essay by Lynda Schneekloth in this volume.

2 _ See James Corner, "Preface," and "Recovering Landscape as a Critical Cultural Practice," in *Recovering Landscape*, ix-xi and 1-26, especially 1-4. For comparison, see François Dagognet, *Mort du paysage? Philosophie et esthétique du paysage* (Seyssel, France: Champ Vallon, 1982).

3 _ On this front, the influence of Ian L. McHarg and his book, *Design with Nature* (Garden City, NY: Natural History Press, 1969), can hardly be overestimated. For a critical perspective on McHarg's approach, see Treib, "Nature Recalled," 30-31.

4 _ Niall Kirkwood, "Reconfigured Ground: Design Practice and Research between landscape and architecture," *Design for the Environment: The*

Interdisciplinary Challenge [ACSA Association of Collegiate Schools of Architecture West Central Regional Conference, 8-6 October 1995] (Champaign, IL: School of Architecture/Building Research Council, University of Illinois at Urbana-Champaign, 1995), 97-104: 97.

5 _ Corner, "Recovering Landscape as a Critical Cultural Practice," 1.

6 _ Bennett, "The Other Side of the Fence," 58.

7 _ See, especially, Anita Berrizbeitia and Linda Pollak, *Inside Outside: between architecture and landscape* (Gloucester, MA: Rockport, 1999), and Charles Waldheim, Landscape Urbanism: A Genealogy, in *Praxis: Journal of Writing + Building 4: Landscape* (2002), 10-17.

8 _ See Ashley Schafer and Amanda Reeser, "Approaching Landscapes," *Praxis* 4 (2002): 4-5: 4, with a quotation from Reynar Banham, *Los Angeles: The Architecture of Four Ecologies* (1971): "Learning from the landscape is a way of being revolutionary for an architect." See also Corner, "Recovering Landscape as a Critical Cultural Practice,"16 and 26, n. 37, concerning explorations at the Architectural Association, London, during the early 1980s.

9 _ Bennett, "The Other Side of the Fence," 58. On the role of historians within design schools, see, especially, Miroslava [Mirka] Beneš, "Teaching History in the School of Design," *GSD News* [Harvard University Graduate School of Design] (Summer 1993): 25-26.

10 _ Corner, "Recovering Landscape as a Critical Cultural Practice," 13-16.

11 _ Treib, "Nature Recalled," 37-41.

12 _ Many thanks to Jim Wescoat for this observation.

13 _ Corner, "Recovering Landscape as a Critical Cultural Practice," 16: "It was not long ago that architects drew the plans and elevations of their build-ings without topographic features, trees, and larger horizons."

14 _ See, for example, the discussion of "highly constructed yet open-ended" in Schafer and Reeser, "Approaching Landscapes," 5.

15 _ See Corner, "Recovering Landscape as a Critical Cultural Practice," 5: "both the idea and the artifact of landscape are not at all static or stable."

16 _ In addition to the publications cited above, especially noteworthy publications include Sanford Kwinter, "Soft Systems," *Culture Lab 1*, ed. Brian Boigon (Princeton, NJ: Princeton Architectural Press, 1993), 207-228; Jan Birksted, ed., *Relating Architecture to Landscape* (New York, NY: E and FN SPON, 1999); David Leatherbarrow, *Uncommon Ground: Architecture, Technology, and Topography* (Cambridge, MA: The MIT Press, 2000); Marc Treib, *The Architecture of Landscape, 1940-1960* (Philadelphia: University of Pennsylvania Press, 2002); Aaron Betsky, *Landscrapers: Building with the Land* (New York, NY: Thames and Hudson, 2002); Journal of Architectural Education (February 2004) "Landscape and Architecture," eds. Vince Canizaro, Kenneth Helphand, and Lynda Schneekloth. Especially noteworthy conferencesinclude "Constructing Landscape" (University of Pennsylvania, 1993); "The Recovery of the Landscape" (Architectural Association, 1994); "Design for the Environment: The Interdisciplinary Challenge" (ACSA West Central Regional Conference, University of Illinois at Urbana-Champaign, 1995); "Landscape" (ACSA West Central Regional Conference on Architecture, University of Kansas, Lawrence, 2001); and "'site out of mind'/Thresholds between Architecture and Landscape Architecture" (University of Virginia, 2004).

17 _ Notable exceptions include Kirkwood, "Reconfigured Ground," *op. cit.*, and Nate Krug, "A Case Study in Collaboration: A Joint Architecture/Landscape Architecture Studio," in *Design for the Environment: The Interdisciplinary Challenge*, 111-114.

18 _ See, especially, Elizabeth B. Kassler, *Modern Gardens and the Landscape* (New York, NY: Museum of Modern Art, 1964); Marc Treib, *Modern Landscape Architecture: A Critical Review* (Cambridge, MA: The MIT Press, 1993); and Treib, *The Architecture of Landscape, 1940-1960, op cit.*

19 _ See Alberto Pérez-Gómez, *Architecture and the Crisis of Modern Science* (Cambridge, MA: The MIT Press, 1983).

20 _ See, for example, Melanie L. Simo, *The Coalescing of Different Forces and Ideas: A History of Landscape Architecture at Harvard, 1900-1999* (Cambridge, MA: Harvard University Graduate School of Design, 2000), and Anthony M. Alofsin, *The Struggle for Modernism: Architecture, Landscape Architecture, and City Planning at Harvard* (New York: W. W. Norton and Company, 2002).

The editor gratefully acknowledges
Brenton and Jean Wadsworth, whose
Wadsworth Endowment Grant
in the Department of Landscape
Architecture, University of Illinois at
Urbana-Champaign, generously sup-
ported all phases in the production
and distribution of this volume.

306090 extends thanks to the Graham
Foundation for Advanced Studies in the
Fine Arts for its support of the publica-
tion of this volume.

During the past year, a substantial number
of students, instructors, and administrators
contacted the editor with reflections about the
theme at hand and information about initiatives
within their programs. Although not named
here, those individuals contributed in significant ways to the shaping of this volume. For
their generosity with time and ideas, the editor
offers many thanks.

Finally, the editor extends personal thanks to
James Wescoat, Dianne Harris, Amita Sinha,
Gerard Bul-lalayao, Patricia McGirr, Kathy
McQuiggan, Jason Johnson, Nataly Gattegno,
Cindy Kennesey, Jennifer Eades, Connie
Coleman, Jonathan Solomon, and Alexander
Briseño for suggestions, advice, research sup-
port, technical assistance, and collegiality.

PROSPECTS

"He who fights the future has a dangerous enemy. The future is not; it borrows its strength from the Man himself and when it has tricked him out of this, then it appears outside him as the enemy he must meet."

///// Søren Kierkegaard

INTEGRATIVE THINKING: ARCHITECTURE AND LANDSCAPE ARCHITECTURE FOR THE NEW MILLENNIUM

James Wines

A sign in the landscape architecture computer lab at Penn State University reads, "think twice, print once." Installed in a desperate attempt to curb students' wasteful use of plotter paper, this cautionary advice to think before acting might be applied to the entire process of design education. In fact, for at least the past twenty years, the teaching of architecture and landscape architecture has been in need of a major re-thinking. With a few luminous exceptions—the legendary Ian McHarg at the University of Pennsylvania being among the most notable—educational practice has been plagued by a regressive, business-as-usual, pattern of redundancy. As a result, the exploration of new ideas, relevant content, and environmental values have been suffocated by the perpetuation of past-due design clichés. As noted in my essay for *Landscape Architecture*, entitled "Connecting the Dots" (November 1999), an already nega- tive situation has been exacerbated by the fact that landscape design suffers from an inferiority complex relative to architecture.[1] Furthermore, it has been forced by the architectural profession to endure a diminished reputation as the backseat driver in urban planning, which, in turn, has created the erroneous public perception of landscape ser- vices as being limited to decoration with plant mate- rials, or tree-hugging activism in the green movement.

As a relatively new arrival at Penn State University—by reason of my appointment to a

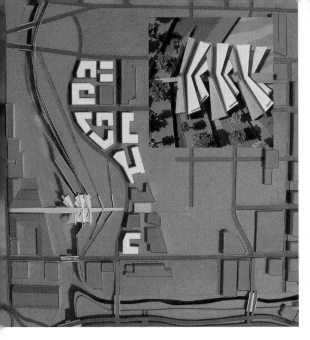 

professorship in architecture—the main attraction to the College of Arts and Architecture, before I arrived, was a declared mobilization toward integrative thinking in architecture and landscape architecture. For two decades I have been profoundly bothered by the unproductive separation of these obviously related disciplines. Furthermore, I have always sought an academic environment where I might help replace the now stale Modernist/Cubist/Constructivist–influenced teaching paradigms with a learning experience where students would be able to expand their creative horizons beyond formalist orthodoxy. I started working on this objective under the enlightened leadership of Anne Spirn, when she chaired landscape architecture in the Graduate School of Fine Arts (GSFA) at the University of Pennsylvania, by developing an integrative educational agenda, which involved collaborations among students of architecture, landscape, urban planning, and visual art. When Anne left her chair position for M.I.T., I tried to continue this interdisciplinary program—modeled after Paul Cret's founding mission statement for the original GSFA—but it was rejected like a cancerous appendage by the subsequent administration. The excuse for cancellation claimed that it complicated budgeting procedures. As I understood this peculiar decision, the promotion of integrative thinking was seen as infinitely less important than maintaining the bureaucratic sanctity of traditional accounting.

Given my disappointing experience at the GSFA, I was overjoyed when I first read former Dean Neil Porterfield's strategic plans for the future of the College of Arts and Architecture at Penn State, which included his strong advocacy for an integration of the arts. Since I discovered sympathetic compatriots and true supporters of progressive design education in both Porterfield and Eliza Pennypacker, I enthusiastically signed on as part of their team.

Clearly, the challenge of promoting integrative thinking as a part of architecture and landscape architecture curricula is not an easy task, especially in the face of a long legacy of separation of the arts in the past century and the kind of hermetic pedagogy that continues to thwart interdisciplinary education. If the Renaissance guild system for arts apprenticeship—for example, the famed Verrocchio Studio in Florence during the 15th Century—can be seen as the most productive archetype for interdisciplinary education, then today's options seem to be a far cry from this model. For example, among the looming threats to the studio-oriented learning environment is the proliferation of "electronic universities." By plugging into net services, the computer user can be comfortably educated at home (even engaging in cyber-space dialogues with design leaders), take examinations, and get a degree without enduring the agony of commuter traffic and the economic drain of attending an expensive institution. On the other hand, as professor Pennypacker points out, "The main attraction to a traditional campus education is the opportunity for peer group dialogue and social interaction." Given the implicit isolation

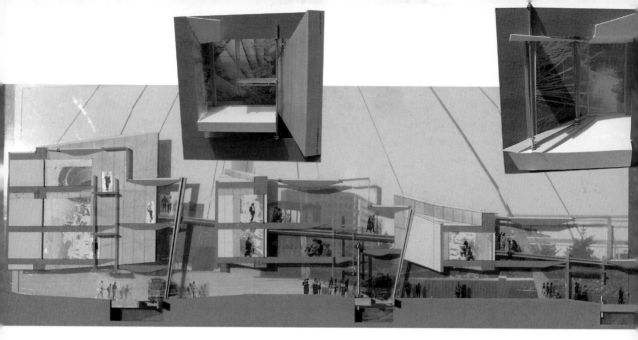

of on-line learning, the lack of direct discourse with student colleagues, and the absence of personal attention from a living/breathing professor, the future of the convivial studio seems still to be assured. A case in point: sometimes when I have been over-burdened with lecture responsibilities, I have tried to cut back on my travel schedule by proposing to send videotapes instead. This offer is invariably rejected because, as one academic colleague put it, "The students are sick of looking at computer screens and want somebody to pinch, pummel and argue with."

The problems of competing with the attractions of internet education are insignificant compared to the sobering checklist of social, economic, ecological, and life-style changes that must be addressed by departments of landscape architecture over the next decade. These include revisions, transformations, even total revolutions in thought that will have an irreversible impact on how the natural environment is perceived and how it will be treated as part of accelerated research within a sustainability scenario.

At the top of this list of priorities is the need for vast reforms in every society's attitudes toward the natural environment. While the landscape architecture profession's credibility is on the rise because of its problem-solving contributions to ecological causes, solutions in the future will ultimately demand deeper societal commitments and basic changes in the economic paradigms for progress. Humanity is presently facing the global threat of a technologically-based catastrophe, or

what Heidegger has referred to as a condition of "debased techne." He proposes that, "When technology has reached this dangerous stage, it lifts Mankind to a level where it confronts problems with which technical thinking is not prepared to cope." It is an unhealthy condition of temporality and resignation that psychically pushes people to a mental point of no return. One perilous result is the seemingly insoluble difficulty green leaders have in persuading the greater population that there is, in fact, a major environmental crisis with life-threatening repercussions. The majority of people still seem to feel that the problem, if it exists at all, is beyond their comprehension and control, so they might as well just ignore it altogether. Since advanced technology is actually at the root of this dilemma, there appears to be no solution.

As a direct consequence of debased techne and its attendant state of denial, there loom the destructive effects of profligate consumption. In response, landscape design curricula must also face the issue of rapidly diminishing resources and the fact that, like architecture, many of its construction methods and land–use conventions are based on the illusion of an infinite supply of fossil fuels. The various resource depletion scenarios should be a required part of landscape education, as a part of fundamental information. Computer-aided research has produced some fairly convincing (and extremely disturbing) predictions for the near future. These databases must be allowed to shape what is taught in colleges and include

speculations on how the built environment will be conceived and maintained in the face of diminishing energy supplies.

Another concern that must be addressed in the teaching syllabi of education is an awareness of the growing tendency for cities to become centers of cultural and recreational activity, while the prime workplace will be the home computer station. It is especially intriguing to speculate on the shape and function of the private house when most of the population will be working out of their living spaces. As it stands now, an additional ten thousand U.S. citizens per year spend most of their time at domestic workstations, with only occasional trips to a company business office for strategy meetings. In fact, many information-based industries are now considering a vast reduction of corporate space in favor of building new cyber-villages, where employees operate primarily out of their home offices. Recalling *company towns* of the early Industrial Revolution, these changes will affect environmental design by forcing landscape architects to re-think urban centers. They will also have to address the issue of new concepts for private gardens, when more and more residential workers will be seeking green space refuge from the burden of having to look at computer monitors all day. The information revolution, like its industrial predecessor at the turn of the century, will inevitably affect design philosophy and, with it, the

entire structure of curricula. It is premature to predict exactly what these revisions will be; but, with early Modernist history as a precedent for radical change, the transformations will surely be dramatic over the next decade.

From an aesthetic perspective and as a result of the dominance of formalist traditions, buildings, environmental technology, and works of landscape architecture are invariably interpreted as separate objects rammed together as uncomfortable bedfellows. One of the main components of integrative thinking will be to reverse this destructive tendency and substitute a learning process where all components are aesthetically and functionally seen as seamless fusions of each other. As Pennypacker has wisely observed, "one of the main benefits of creative interaction and outreach communication is that they eliminate misconceptions of other disciplines based on ignorance."

In line with this critique of formalist baggage—which usually limits the interpretation of design to the manipulation of shapes, volumes and spaces for their own sake—both architecture and landscape architecture must be opened up to the full breadth of art experience of the past century. In general, the profession has missed out on the rich sources of content to be found in social and psychological situations, the notion of art as a mental (rather than formal/physical) experience, the use of context as a generator of ideas, and the human

body as an intrinsic part of the designed environment. In particular, with all of the preference for vast expanses of hardscape in contemporary public space design, this situation has neglected the prosthetic presence—referring to the importance of human scale, kinetic interaction among people, and the relation of the individual parts of the body to context. Too many buildings and civic spaces undervalue the social and psychological impact, resulting from the successful orchestration of sight, smell, touch, hearing, and movement.

Another neglected issue is the question of how architecture and landscape architecture will embrace cultural diversity. In a social structure like that of the U.S., it is unconscionable for virtually all buildings and spaces only to reflect Euro-centric legacies, while ignoring the vast range of ethnic and cultural influences that have been responsible for vitality in every other facet of social, economic, and artistic achievement. This state of denial ties in with a growing disregard for the individual in community life and the rejection of non-institutional values in environmental design. There is much lip service given to the need for multicultural identity in the built environment, but little action to address this omission, when reflected in design practice.

The list of aberrations in environmental design goes on, but one final problem that still remains paramount is modern society's total elimination of urban agriculture and rooftop green space in contemporary cities. Simply by absorbing some lessons from the ancient world, where every truly productive metropolis was conceived as a reflection of the interactive models found in nature, one can see the value of integrating the built with the green. At the opposite extreme today, for example, we have the ecologically devastating absurdity of plunking all the cornfields in concentrated regions (where, among other deficits, they attract every species of corn predator to converge and devour). As an alternative, landscape architecture education can perform at least one valuable service by focusing its research on new ideas for garden cities.

It is no secret that I am committed to the idea of integrative education in both architecture and landscape architecture. The changes I propose are as follows:

• The main objective is to develop an interdisciplinary model for education that involves genuine teamwork among landscape architects, architects, artists, psychologists, scientists, and any other logically related disciplines. While this is not a new idea by any means, it usually fails in academia because the collaborations are self-consciously conceived as exotic experiments, not as intrinsic features of curricula. These showcase situations inevitably become awkward confrontations and often end up generating combative games for individual supremacy. The only successful approach is to develop the kind of studio projects that make combined expertise an imperative component for achieving results. This process also favors learning by doing, as opposed to classroom lessons in professional practice.

• Start the entire architecture and landscape design educational sequence by learning about the relationships between habitat and environment, before it became the highly organized product of economic systems and stylistic interventions. For example, by studying Neolithic and Aboriginal cultures—particularly their concepts of living *with* nature—this information can have a lingering impact on a student's subsequent thinking about the balance between ecology and construction.

• Use the "learning by doing" model (like the Renaissance workshop) to connect design with construction technology, history, and theory in a flowing continuum throughout all sequential years of education. This refers to the assignment of studio problems that address urgent and realistic community issues and involve outside professional advisors whenever possible. Avoid the usual peda-gogical compartmentalizing that tends to isolate ideas and processes from problem solving, professionalism and hands-on action.

• Teach all architecture and landscape architecture as an extension of the full measure of natural phenomena—not simply horticulture and design—by including such inspirational forces as psychology, sociology, ecology, anatomy, biophysics, astrophysics, cosmology, political science, and green technology. Exposure to the widest range of sources can only enrich the learning process and provide more varied and potent sources of design ideas. The point is to avoid teaching the conventional twentieth-century bag of stylistic tricks that only thwart student creativity and perpetuate the erroneous impression that style can be substituted for content.

Pennypacker, Porterfield, and I have frequently discussed the future of architecture and landscape architecture at Penn State and our challenge is embodied in Pennypacker's fundamental question; "We know that we need to be interdisciplinary; but do we really have the passion to do it?" She continues, "We also understand that we need to be more environmentally sensitive; but we still don't quite achieve our goals. We treat the problem like the eight glasses of water a day we know we are supposed to drink, or the one hour of exercise we

are supposed to perform. Somehow the recognition of what is good for us never quite manifests itself in action." There is always a vast difference between the unstoppable compulsion actually to create new and revolutionary art, versus the intellectual dialogue that merely defines need and speculates about solutions. Unfortunately, the academic environment tends to encourage the latter. This is not always the case, however. The Architectural Association in London, under the brilliant leadership of the late Alvin Boyarsky during the 1970s and 80s, generated a hot bed of revolutionary exploration and energy. Through their roles as either students or teachers—including, for example, Peter Cook, Dennis Crompton, Zaha Hadid, Rem Koolhaas, Bernard Tschumi, as well as a continuous stream of visiting luminaries—the AA became identified with an entire generation of cutting edge art and design activity. But Alvin Boyarsky didn't actually create this explosion; he just gave it a nurturing environment in which to thrive.

It is always dangerous to try to predict whether there will be a seminal surge of innovation in any field and what form this might take. The problem is that one can sometimes foresee certain needs, but also be totally off base in terms of prophesies for the shape of solutions. I feel certain that every architecture and landscape architecture program in this country is experiencing the pressures I have described above, and most academic activists are developing plans to address the challenges to traditional education. Still, success can never be achieved by the lip service of leadership (or essays like this), even though key issues need to be defined before any revolution can take place. As Alvin Boyarsky used to say about educational institutions, "the real creativity is still in the hands of the people you hire to serve under your roof." I would add to this statement Pennypacker's ultimate question, "do we really have the passion to do it?"

James Wines *is a Professor in the Department of Architecture at Penn State. He is founder, president, and creative director of SITE, a New York–based architecture and environmental arts organization.*

NOTES

1 _ See James Wines, "Connecting the Dots" [Critic at Large], *Landscape Architecture* (November 1999): 170-172.

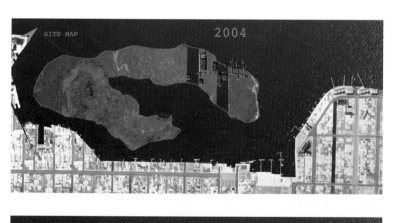

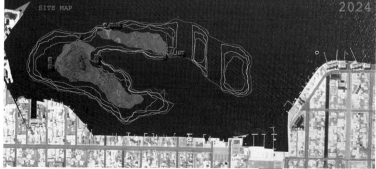

A conversation format / w/ Björn
is landscape format / & Alexander

i.e.
Aven / Yale ⟶ want a plan working as [typo / morpho...]

⟶ expansion of objects to include

PASSPORT

EXTENDED OBJECT (OWN SPACE/SIZE) (COMPLEXITY FORMAL)
BIGITAL MANIPULATIONS

various
scale
(DIFFERENT USES)

TIME / STATEST

Eng.
XIX c.
RESTORATION/DEV. INTEGRATED

secondary (vert.)

PARADOX

[ETHNOGRAPHICAL
PARADIGM]

ground (horiz.)
Sculpt
XIX c.

architecture //
←→
(art. architecture)
LANDSCAPE

BLURRING?

FORMAT,

user
Stein = expand ready/scale
size

landscape
surfaces (region/open space)

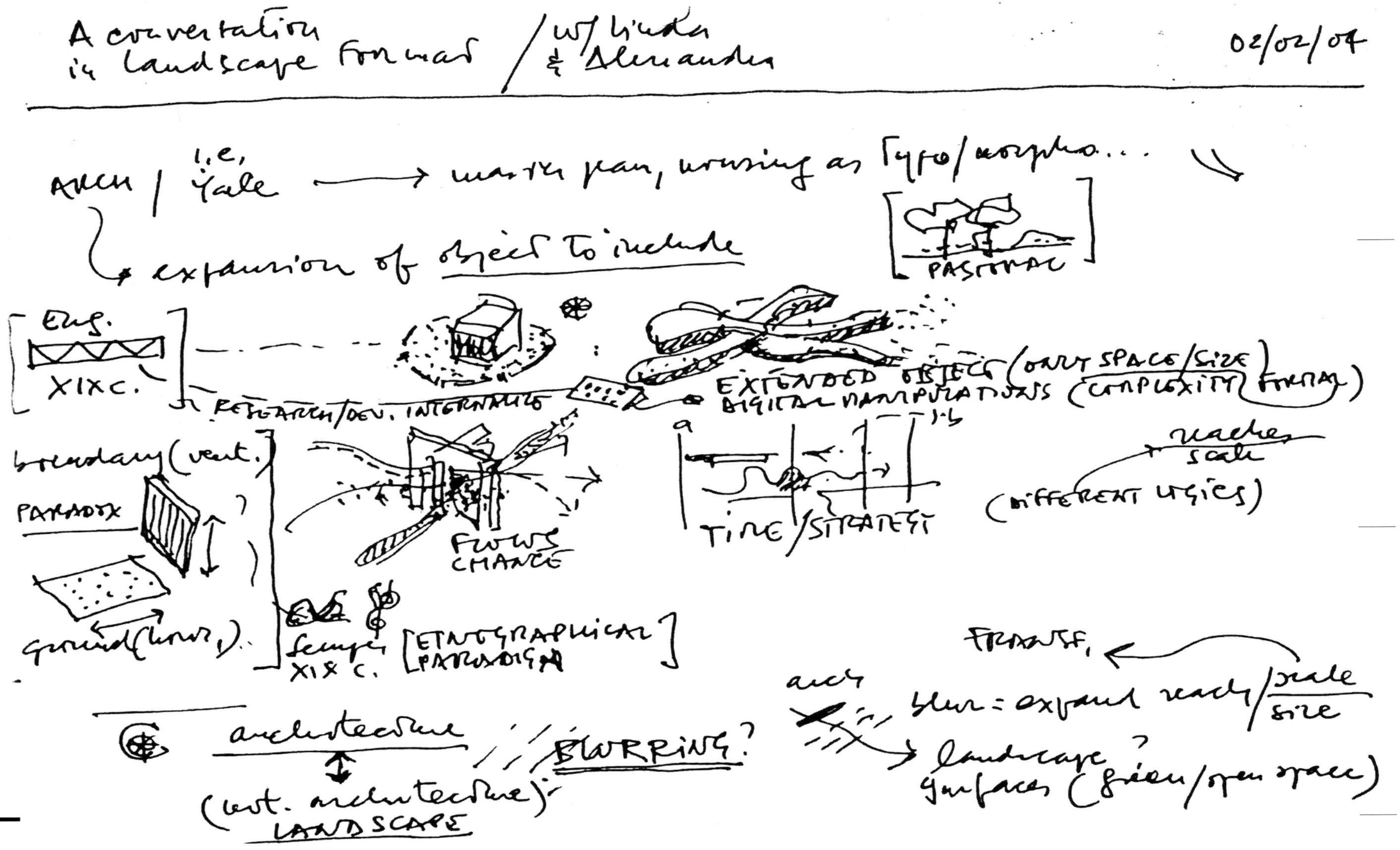

AND: TEACHING LANDSCAPE IN ARCHITECTURE

(DISCUSSION 01/25/04)

Alessandra Ponte, Sandro Marpillero, and Linda Pollak

Alessandra Ponte/////I have been in a number of final reviews recently, in different schools of architecture. The object is dissolving. Many studio critics are assigning or working with landscape themes at the moment.

Sandro Marpillero/////It is not that the object is dissolving in the work you are referring to. Usually it is just getting bigger, going from object to extended object.

Linda Pollak/////There is nothing inherently wrong with landscape becoming an object. Yet the objects in question tend to be weak, because they are constructed almost entirely in formal terms. They are big beautiful things, without much resistance.

AP/////The students know little about landscape, so they are forced to invent when they don't need to. In one jury, for a studio on a vast urban project, a student had a large area of outdoor space. I asked what it was and she said it was a park. In response to "What is a park?" she answered, "a surface." In a different jury, also for an urban scale project, a student was struggling with the presence of abandoned buildings, trying to elaborate an aesthetic of ruins without being aware of three centuries of theories on the subject, including the Picturesque, from William Gilpin to Robert

Images by Mary Miss.
Rosalind E.Krauss,
"Sculpture in the
Expanded Field," *The
Originality of the
Avant-Garde and Other
Modernist Myths*, The
MIT Press, 1986, pp. 276.

Smithson. So…the students need more understanding of landscape. They are given projects with landscape themes but without a background on the western and non-western culture of the landscape. They are un-prepared from this point of view.

SM/////Landscape is more than not-architecture. Many architects and architecture students talk about blurring, yet to blur is to let what used to be accepted as a boundary become less clear. Projects expand and attempt to control more territory, without necessarily having the techniques to address different scales.

LP/////For architecture to engage issues of landscape in architecture requires the calibration

of different scales in relationship to each other, rather than a shift to a larger scale. Part of the challenge is how to enable architects to engage a site, without becoming so overwhelmed by it that it dominates, or so attached to it that they cannot allow themselves to imagine how to alter it. I used to offer architecture studios focusing on nature in the city, but these projects tended to generate a lot of sentimentality about the supposed naturalness of a place. In more recent studios focusing on cultural institutions, the transformation of an existing industrial building can engage an urban landscape at multiple scales, in tension with a cultural stance.

AP/////I would like to go back to what Sandro said about landscape being more than "not-architecture" and discuss the "expanded field" theorized by Rosalind Krauss in her famous essay on sculpture, one of the few readings on contemporary issues about landscape given to students in architecture. I want to reference two texts. Neither has anything to do with landscape, but they suggest interesting critical alternatives.

The first is a book by Derrida, *Given Time.*[1] Part of it is a commentary on the famous essay on the gift by Marcel Mauss. Derrida explains how Mauss analyzed systems of exchange in almost a structural way, but without ever losing sight of the thing itself. Mauss insisted in particular on the Maori concept of *hau*, the spirit of things, to show how "What imposes obligation in the present received and exchanged, is the fact that the thing received is not inactive. Even when it has been abandoned by the giver, it still possesses something of him […] the *hau* follows after anyone possessing the thing."[2] Derrida emphasizes this focus on the aura of the thing exchanged, dismissing the critique of the role of the hau advanced by Claude Lévi-Strauss in his *Introduction to the Work of Marcel Mauss.*[3] According to Derrida, Lévi-Strauss eliminates all question of the difficulties regarding the intrinsic value of the gift by substituting a pure logic of relation of exchange for the notion of *hau*. In so doing, Lévi-Strauss causes to vanish even the very value of the gift. In extending this sort of criticism to the structuralist approach of Lévi-Strauss in general, one may observe that Levi-Strauss's diagrams succeed in building a system

LP/////Yet, each of us is describing a level of precision that you don't obtain if you assume that either "landscape" or "architecture" has some self evident meaning. It is more productive to acknowledge that each of them has its own histories, meanings, and nuances of meaning.

SM/////This term "histories" has a lot to do with how one approaches the teaching of studio. By setting up a relationship between a project and a site, one acknowledges that the site itself carries not only an official history—that which is usually visible and perceivable, described in maps and other representations—but also other histories, which have been repressed. In general, attention to a site is not about searching for the gold nugget, a "spirit" of the place, to be treated as another item in the brief. It has more to do with being aware that history with a big H belongs to the interests of those who won and therefore were able to impose a certain representation of reality.

LP/////In a studio I recently taught focusing on a multimedia center in Chelsea, the students found out that the building was built in the 1930s to store ice, as part of an industrial framework from a certain time, which produced a particular scale of space. This specificity made it possible to see the building's own layers, its lining, its connections to other buildings and to the city in a way that was more potent than assuming it to be a generic loft space. Making a connection between the building and an adjacent elevated rail system built at the same time, to bring perishable foods to the city, served to introject an urban landscape scale within the building itself.

SM/////A landscape approach, because it engages almost imperceptible processes, implies that what is significant is precisely what is happening at the scale of minute contradictions that are emerging or becoming or barely visible or repressed. Not everything moves according to a trajectory of manifestation; things also move along trajectories of disappearance. The clues, and therefore also the possibilities, lie precisely at such moments of contradiction. One can think about practice or studio as an attempt to bring to full material tangibility or consistency latent possibilities embedded in a situation, vis a vis a certain

desire on the part of a designer which invests that particular situation with a thrust or a trajectory. It is precisely such embedded possibilities that can have a tremendous effect on the redefinition of the desire itself.

To be honest I do not make much difference between landscape and the city

AP/////I don't either.

LP/////Yet each term comes with a set of assumptions.

SM/////It is helpful to understand the term landscape, as James Corner has clarified, less from within a pictorial tradition and more in the Dutch tradition of *landschaft*, which carries within its historical genesis embedded traces of human labor, reflecting the degree to which, in Holland, every square inch is gained from the water, and therefore has been worked on, and therefore is an expression of material culture. If one extends this line of thinking to subsume or reframe the classic juxtaposition between the city and nature according to an interest in, or commitment to, material culture…this is also what an architect does, in that s/he is trying to produce something that is culturally relevant out of the simple fact that one is asked to design something in order to put together bricks and/or other materials in a particular moment. Architecture can be understood as something that is not commodifiable to the degree to which it is reinscribed into both material culture and processes of ecological transformation, whether the site is the city or a field. Quite frankly, the countryside is marked, grooved, and worked, and carries an immense amount of traces, and cities are replete with biotic processes.

AP/////I don't tell my students this sort of thing anymore. I say, "This is the title of the seminar: "landscape and architecture." I expect you to know about architecture, and I will explain to you what landscape is."

SM/////You risk leaving unquestioned the typological tradition of architecture, to the degree to which typology is that which gets to be coagulated or crystallized as a sort of common essence of

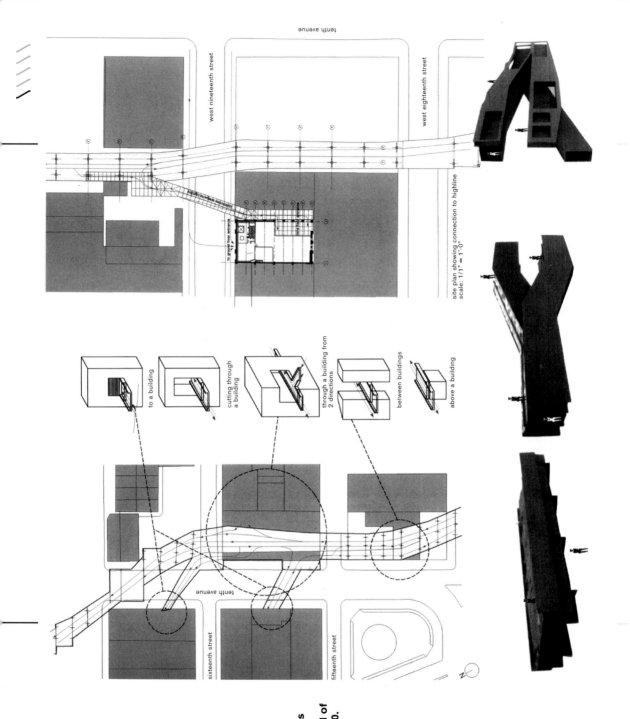

tenth avenue

west nineteenth street

west eighteenth street

site plan showing connection to highline
scale: 1/1" = 1'-0"

to a building

cutting through
a building

through a building from
2 directions

between buildings

above a building

tenth avenue

sixteenth street

fifteenth street

N

Work by Gustavo Garcia.
STUDIOWORKS 10: Options
Thesis Research, Harvard
University Graduate School of
Design 2001-2003, pp. 15-20.

behavior in history—as if history and monuments could be translated into a foundation for an architectural work, or as if a city could be reduced to morphological variations on a figure ground pattern. It is precisely such a process of ossification that precludes the approaches we are discussing.

In teaching the first semester studio of Urban Design at Columbia, my attempt, with Andrea Kahn, has been to communicate to the students that: a) design is not bad, and b) one does not revert to a quantitative approach as a response to the corruption of [the idea of] quality by the commodification of urban space. The Columbia program challenges this polarity between a statistical, political, not-formal world on the one hand, and an aesthetic formal one on the other, that characterizes much of urban design teaching. In the context of Columbia, where a landscape department does not exist, we have worked to integrate landscape issues and landscape architecture critics, as part of a program through which to approach urban design in other than formal terms.

LP/////An architecture studio that can include landscape architecture students must be flexible enough to accommodate people who do not have a background in architecture, without being wide open. For example, the fall studio I taught last year on the SculptureCenter in Long Island City focused on issues of topography in three parts: first, the transformation of the interior of an existing industrial building; second, a transformation of the building's disjunctive urban situation; and third, a substantial addition to the building. Each student had to do all three parts—the first two, which occurred simultaneously, and then the addition, which became the primary project for the architects, occupying the second half of the semester, but played a minor role for the landscape architects, who, after several weeks, returned to the urban landscape project as their primary focus. The landscape students' encounter with an architectural framework strengthened their approach to the urban landscape, whereas the architects' encounter with issues of landscape strengthened their approach to the architecture of the addition.

In pedagogical terms, it's great to have students from various disciplines together in a studio or seminar. If architects have contact with landscape architects in a studio context, they can begin to understand how a project is framed and approached, that it is more than folded horizontal surfaces. The architects benefit from exposure to a different sensibility as well as the landscape architects' familiarity with different resources such as GIS and topographical mapping. And vice versa. In other words, it is possible to deploy the simultaneous presence of students of different disciplines performatively, to draw out issues by exploiting differences in the students' knowledge base, in collaboration with them, to enrich the studio experience. Such an encounter between disciplines has the potential to enlarge architecture's scope and capacity, yet also makes it clear that it is not possible to enlarge this scope endlessly. One has to find ways of cutting through or across.

Acknowledging that they (don't) know different things can be a catalyst for students to collaborate across disciplines. For instance, a landscape architect might be able to conceive of and manipulate a surface, yet s/he would have a difficult time disengaging from it, to make a quasi-discrete artifact, which would conversely be easier for the architect.

AP/////We have to teach landscape to architecture students. Because landscape has really been evacuated from architecture, for over a century. And architecture is not part of the teaching of landscape.

LP/////Architecture hasn't always been evacuated from landscape architecture—if you think about the work of Garrett Eckbo, for instance—just as landscape considerations haven't always been evacuated from architecture—thinking, for instance, about Richard Neutra. Le Corbusier did fascinating things with landscape, but he didn't theorize or write about it.

At Harvard, architecture students can take courses in the Department of Landscape Architecture, which often affect their thinking profoundly. Yet, I think that what we are talking about is a specific position of teaching about landscape in an architectural curriculum. You know that your students are interested in landscape; you want to empower them to go beyond a superficial level in their explorations, to engage a set of practices. The fact that architects want to appropriate landscape themes, yet are for the most part uninterested in the discipline of landscape architecture, is a complex issue.

AP/////There are different ways of studying landscape.

LP/////As with architecture, it is not productive to generalize: landscape architecture is taught in different ways at different schools.

In writing *Inside Outside: between architecture and landscape* with Anita [Berrizbeitia],[5] I played more or less the role of the architect, she that of the landscape architect. I became aware that her approach was more attuned to looking for change. The notion of "operation" allowed us

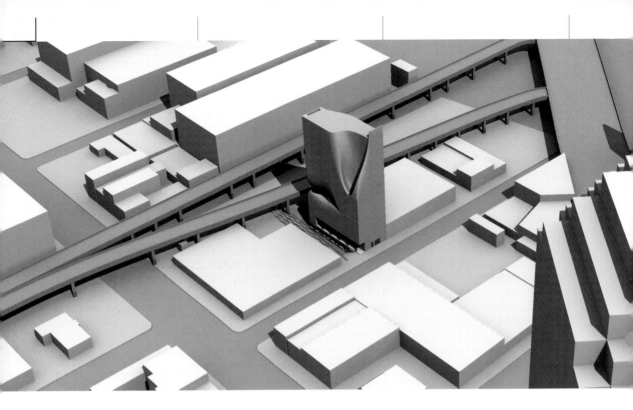

to invent ways of framing dynamic relationships between landscape and architecture. Teaching with Sandro in Jim Corner's department of Landscape Architecture at Penn has allowed us to attain a more fine-grained understanding of some aspects of mapping and layering different kinds of knowledge or forces and flows associated with landscape.

Part of the problem with the way that landscape is currently thematized in architecture, is the way in which it is depoliticized. The history of landscape reveals its use to naturalize power, by representing its own innocence, claiming naturalness. To go back to Alessandra's anecdote about a park being understood only as a surface: it is important for the designer to engage the representation of nature in cities, as well as the encounter with natural elements. How do you address issues of landscape and ideology in this context?

AP/////These issues do matter. For instance, what is a public park? It is difficult to explain to students that what they are thinking of as a public park is a nineteenth-century public park, that what they think is reality is a construction.

Alessandra Ponte, *Dip. Arch., Ph.D., is an Associate Professor at the Pratt Institute.* **Sandro Marpillero**, *M.Arch., M.Sci. (Architecture and Building Design), and* **Linda Pollak**, *M.Arch., MLA, are founding principals of Marpillero Pollak Architects, a practice based in New York City. Marpillero is an Adjunct Associate Professor in the Columbia Graduate School of Architecture and a lecturer in the Department of Architecture at the University of Pennsylvania. Pollak is a Design Critic at the Graduate School of Design, Harvard.*

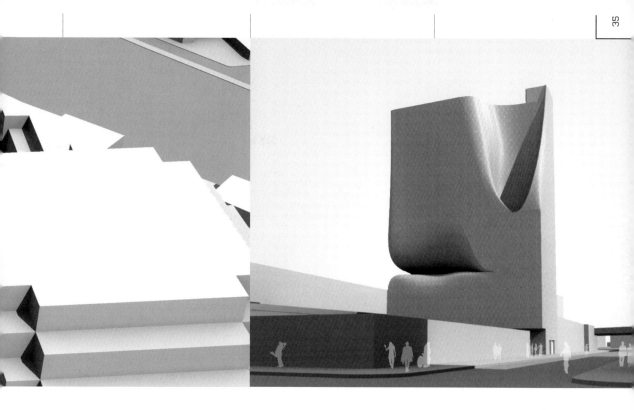

Works by Liam O'Brien. SC:LIC, SculptureCenter, Long Island City, Harvard University Graduate School of Design, 2003.

NOTES

1 _ Jacques Derrida, *Given Time: I. Counterfeit Money*, (Chicago/London: University of Chicago Press, 1992).

2 _ Marcel Mauss, *The Gift* [*Essai sur le Don, 1950*] (New York and London: W.W. Norton, 1990), 11-12.

3 _ Claude Lévi-Strauss, *Introduction to the Work of Marcel Mauss*, trans. Felicity Baker (London: Routledge and Kegan Paul, 1987).

4 _ Gilles Deleuze, "Trois Questions sur Six Fois Deux (Godard)", *Pourparlers (1972-1990)*, (Paris: Les Éditions de Minuit, 1990), 55-66.

5 _ Anita Berrizbeita and Linda Pollak, *Inside Outside: between architecture and landscape* (Gloucester, MA: Rockport, 2003).

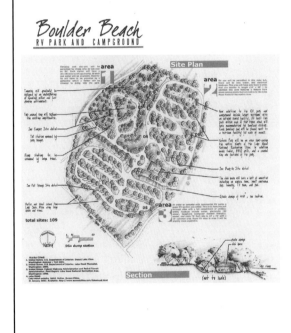

Boulder Beach
RV PARK AND CAMPGROUND

We also currently have a cooperative agreement with the National Park Service to provide design services at the Lake Mead National Recreation Area. Past and current services to the LMNRA include redesign of:

- The Boulder Beach Campground,
- Echo Bay concessionaire and NPS facilities,
- Cottonwood Cove camping and picnic facilities,
- Hemenway beach facilities,
- The Redstone Picnic Area,
- Three trailheads (Wetlands, Bluggs, and River Mountain), and
- Blue Point Springs Amenities.

Lake Mead National Recreation Area (LMNRA).

Through a Memorandum of Understanding, the National Park Service sponsors student projects at a number of scales at LMNRA. In addition, students work as interns for the park before and after graduation. Land management agencies express keen interest in student and faculty assistance from landscape architecture programs because those programs integrate understanding of natural systems with social, cultural, and form-giving skills.

THE CENTRALITY OF LAND-BASED ISSUES IN DESIGN EDUCATION: ARCHITECTURE WITHIN LANDSCAPE

Mark Hoversten

The relationship between architecture and landscape architecture appears to be an increasingly popular topic among educators in the design disciplines. Witness the February 2004 issue of the *Journal of Architectural Education*, entitled "Landscape and Architecture,"[1] or the 2004 Woltz Symposium at the University of Virginia, featuring the evocative title "Thresholds between Architecture and Landscape Architecture." Architects as divergent in disposition as James Wines and Marc Treib have published widely on this relationship. Much of the dialogue has been limited to garden design, perhaps because, among the many niches comprised within landscape architecture, gardens correspond most directly with architecture in terms of scale, concern for form, materials, and a recognizable stylistic imprint of the designer. Nevertheless, the current interest is not new. It is, instead, part of a longer and more generalized, though no less intense, effort to formulate a theoretical base for landscape architecture as a discipline and to situate that base in relation to the already established rubric of art and architectural theory. That history dates back at least to Garrett Eckbo's earliest writings in *Pencil Points* and his appeal for more landscape architectural research in the 1950s and 1960s. Starting in the early 1980s the Council of Educators in Landscape Architecture (CELA) began publishing *Landscape Journal*, a periodical dedicated to "dissemination of the results of academic research and scholarly investigation" dealing with "design, planning and management of the land." Several recent efforts to codify those results have moved Eckbo's dream closer to reality.[2] On the basis of this ongoing dialogue, I believe that the relationship identified in the title of this volume—landscape within architecture—should be reversed. That is to say, architecture lies within landscape because land-based issues are central to the challenges facing design education. Let me explain.

The Centrality of Land-Based Issues in Shaping our Future

Education in general, and design education as a subset of it, should engage issues facing humanity. Design education should be shaped in large part by how we address land-based challenges because those are far and away the most pressing issues designers will face in the next generation. Although there are many examples that might be considered, I will discuss three to suggest how our approach to architectural education must change. Those challenges are environmental damage, urban growth and healthy cities, and the aesthetics of place. I believe that landscape architecture as a discipline offers design education in general the most useful model and the greatest hope for success.

Environmental Damage. Most designers agree that we face increasingly serious environmental challenges that must be addressed by design solutions. Ecologists teach us that those challenges are complex and interrelated. For example, air quality is greatly impacted by transportation planning which, in turn, influences surface water quality. The design and management of surface water systems, on the other hand, determines to a great degree how much fresh water is available for human use, as well as where and to whom it is available. At the same time, wetlands and riparian areas tend to foster higher biological diversity and often act as wildlife corridors. The web of connected issues goes on and on. An understanding of natural sciences such as biology, hydrology, climate, and geology, as well as an understanding of the human imprint on the land—all standard components of landscape architectural education—are required in order to manipulate matter for human use while minimizing damage to natural systems and maximizing availability of resources. All design professionals—including architects—are accountable to these issues.

Urban Growth and Healthy Cities. Rapid urban growth at the fringes of metropolitan areas consumes arable land, wildlife habitat, surface water retention areas (again, wetlands), and

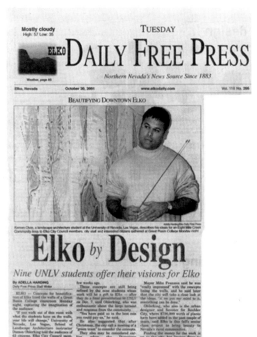

Elko by Design.

Each year, a number of land management agencies support fourth-year landscape architecture and planning studios that prepare plans for small, rural communities throughout the state. Among those agencies are the Nevada Division of Forestry, the Natural Resources Conservation Service, the Bureau of Recreation, and the National Park Service. These plans generate approximately $50,000 of in-kind services per class used by the community as local match for implementation grants. UNLV interns provide community assistance with grant writing, plan refinement, preparation of RFP's, and community events.

recreational zones. The scope and size of urban growth, as well as its negative impact on neighborhood character, are greatly increased by current transportation and land planning that consumes large amounts of land, makes people dependent upon the automobile for virtually all aspects of life, and divides neighborhoods by relatively high speed roads. These, in turn, have contributed to alarming increases in obesity as exercise is removed from daily life patterns. Like environmental challenges, urban design challenges today require an approach that integrates natural systems with social, cultural and form-giving skills. They also require the ability to comprehend those systems at a broad range of scales, so that relationships between regional- and site-scale impacts are considered. Again, these issues are already being addressed in our schools by landscape architectural education.

The Aesthetics of Place. Aside from the challenges mentioned above, the land—in the largest sense of that term—shapes our sense of place—in the largest sense of *that* term. Much has been written about Western civilization's alienation from nature.[3] Nature controlled in urban environments offers little to ground us in a specific place and time. Inordinate amounts of time spent viewing computers, television, and movies further remove us from the place where we live. Although the ecological and financial costs are high, the spiritual costs are higher. We live in a place, but we are not *of* it. Because we don't experience our unique natural environments, we are left without a sense of place and are without an identity. Place provides a common denominator in people's lives.

Implications for Architectural Education

Although architectural form is a necessary component of the solution to each of these challenges, the latter are not primarily issues of form. Rather, they are based in the land, and landscape architecture as a discipline addresses them most directly and intensely. Because of their education, landscape architects offer skills integrating natural systems- and site-engineering into the social, cultural, and form-giving aspects of design. Because they work at scales ranging from regions to specific sites, they place questions of urban design into richer and more appropriate contexts. Because they specialize in knowing the land, the palette with which they work connects people to the earth. With that in mind, I recommend three simple yet far reaching changes to design education.

Nevada Department of Transportation (NDOT). Through sponsored grants, UNLV prepared NDOT's first Landscape and Aesthetics Master Plan, establishing high-level vision and policies, planning and design procedures, design guidelines, and state funding. The project changed the way NDOT views highways throughout the state and resulted in $5 million in private sector consulting during the first five years. Currently, UNLV provides research support for preparation of implementation procedures and review of detailed project design. The landscape architect's ability to comprehend systems at a broad range of scales assures that both regional- and site-scale impacts are considered.

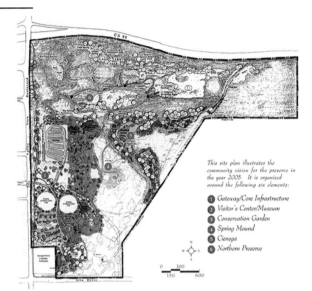

This site plan illustrates the
community vision for the preserve in
the year 2005. It is organized
around the following six elements:

1 *Gateway/Core Infrastructure*
2 *Visitor's Center/Museum*
3 *Conservation Garden*
4 *Spring Mound*
5 *Cienega*
6 *Northern Preserve*

0   300
  150   600

Las Vegas Springs Preserve.

UNLV created the original vision for this 180-acre interpretive facility dedicated to understanding Las Vegas' past and suggesting more sustainable alternatives for its future. For eight years, UNLV landscape architecture and planning faculty coordinated research biologists, archaeologists, and historians as well as private sector planning, interpretive, and design teams. The facility will open in 2005. An understanding of natural sciences such as biology, hydrology, climate, and geology, as well as an understanding of the human imprint on the land, enabled landscape architects to envision and articulate the project to a wide audience.

Adjust School Missions to Respond to the Local Landscape. Not every architecture program can or should specialize in its regional landscape, but a significant number must if architecture is to remain relevant. In order to respond consciously to the local landscape, schools can change their hiring practices as well as their curricula. Faculty chosen because of their commitment to and knowledge of the landscape will inevitably reflect different sets of values and establish closer ties to landscape architecture. Environmental controls and building materials courses can most easily respond to questions of local climate and materials. But architectural students should also take landscape architecture courses, and not just plant materials courses. Courses can be cross-listed or team taught as long as the content and teaching is truly land-based rather than simply inviting landscape architects to join normative architecture courses and vice versa.

Increase the Number of Landscape Architecture Graduates. Landscape architecture is facing a critical shortage of professionals while, at the same time, the number of graduates is slightly decreasing.[4] Consequently, outstanding career opportunities exist in landscape architecture, and average salaries are higher than those of architects.[5] Yet, anecdotal analysis of architecture seems to indicate a surplus of architectural graduates each year as compared to job availability. Given the reduction in legislative funding during the past few years, increasing the number of landscape architecture graduates has proven problematic. In order to address land-based issues and provide an adequate supply of professionals, schools might reduce the number of architecture graduates in order to convert resources to landscape architecture. Furthermore, schools might encourage graduates with a Bachelor of Architecture to pursue the Master of Landscape Architecture as their graduate degree. Finally, more landscape architectural programs are needed.

Change Educational Culture and Leadership. The title of this volume, "Landscape within Architecture," alludes to a common notion within schools of design that landscape and landscape architecture are auxiliary to architecture. Because that idea is pervasive and so-often assumed, it is often invisible to architecture students. A subliminal lesson is learned and the value attached to it is absorbed. The notion impacts every aspect of educational culture from scheduling of courses, to hiring practices, to enrollment management, to funding priorities.

I argue that this assumption serves poorly those who depend on us to help solve problems. For example, eighty-seven percent of Nevada—the state in which I teach—is owned by the federal government. Four of our communities rank among the fastest growing in the nation, whereas the remainder of small towns economically dependent on extraction industries are rapidly losing population. Several national parks, several American Indian reservations, the notorious Area 51, the nuclear test site, the "loneliest highway," the remnants of the Sagebrush Revolution, and a cowboy poetry festival can all be found within the state. Public agencies have looked to landscape architecture and planning—our program has returned to its original historical mandate by reuniting these disciplines—to solve their problems. As a result, we have provided approximately $1.5 million in pre-design and pre-planning research over the past ten years. That research resulted in over $12 million in private sector consulting fees. More importantly, it has provided needed academic, research-based, and objective pre-design and pre-planning services that integrate natural sciences, cultural and social issues, form-giving, and management policy. In so doing, we have extended our educational mission to public agencies and the private sector by bringing research-based ideas into play throughout the state.

The notion of landscape as a subset or auxiliary of architecture serves students and faculty poorly as well. Our students have gained valuable experience, not to mention well-paying jobs, and are prepared for careers in public practice. They have been exposed to a myriad of scientists, public agency managers, and the best consultant teams in the nation. We are now instituting an internship policy in which we place students into these agencies following graduation. The students will jump start careers, while the state will train its own core of public practitioners. The success of this approach testifies to its relevance. Although Landscape Architecture and Planning is the smallest program in the School of Architecture, the program leads the School in numbers of national student and faculty design awards, peer-reviewed publications, sponsored research, faculty recognition, and national service.

A change in educational culture will open the ranks of leadership positions such as design school deanships to more landscape architects.[6] A development of that sort would help foster dialogue among programs and better understanding in general of the land-based issues that are an inevitable part of our future.

Mark Hoversten, *FASLA, AICP, is Professor and Coordinator of Landscape Architecture and Planning at the University of Nevada's School of Architecture. His research focuses on issues of the Mojave Desert and Intermountain West. He currently serves as president of the Council of Educators in Landscape Architecture and is a trustee of the Red Rock Canyon Interpretive Association.*

The author thanks Susan B. Jones, Research Associate at the University of Nevada at Las Vegas, for her helpful review of this essay prior to submittal.

NOTES

1 _ Lynda Schneekloth, Vincent B. Canizaro, and Kenneth Helphand, eds., Special Issue: "Landscape and Architecture," *Journal of Architectural Education* 57: 3 (2004).

2 _ See, for example, Mark Francis and Randolph T. Hester, Jr., eds., *The Meaning of Gardens: Idea, Place, and Action* (Cambridge, MA.: The MIT Press, 1999), and Simon Swaffield, ed., *Theory in Landscape Architecture: A Reader* (Philadelphia, PA: The University of Pennsylvania Press, 2002).

3 _ See, for example, Robert L. Thayer, Jr., *Grey World, Green Heart: Technology, Nature, and the Susatainable Landscape* (New York, NY: Wiley, 1994), and James Howard Kunstler, *The Geography of Nowhere: the Rise and Decline of America's Man-made Landscape* (New York, NY: Simon & Schuster, 1994).

4 _ Karen Hanna, "Challenges in Education 2002," presented to the President's Council: ALSA, CELA, CLARB, LAAB, LAF (2002).

5 _ *National Salary Survey of Landscape Architects 1998* (Washington, D.C.: American Society of Landscape Architects, 1998).

4 _ At the time of writing, only six members of ASLA hold the rank of dean at schools of design in the United States. Only four of them are landscape architects.

Donald Judd, Marfa, Texas, 2002. (photo: Jessie Marshall)

THE CULTIVATION OF SITE: LANDSCAPE APPROACHES IN THE TEACHING OF ARCHITECTURE

Jessie Marshall

Shimmering against the bright sky, Donald Judd's huge concrete boxes—cast in the open plain at Marfa—seem to determine the Texas horizon. The rhythm of the boxes—human height, with black shadows thrown hard against shocking sun—alters the perception of field and sky, inscribing a walking pace of passage onto the expansive openness. Reflective, layered, and measured experience of place is conveyed with powerful specificity. Recently arrived from Europe, lost in both the Texas plains and the suburban endlessness of Dallas, I recognized here a rhythm in the desert landscape.

Architectural education in Texas retains a strong legacy from Colin Rowe. The curricular framework, developed from the influential 1954 University of Texas discourse on space and structure, is condensed in the teaching studio through compositional lessons from collage and analytic cubism—solid and void, balance and juxtaposition—creating a language of architectural abstraction. Within that teaching approach, "the appreciation or precedent of object or figure is assumed to require the presence of some sort of ground field."[1] Furthermore, according to Rowe and Fred Koetter, "when figure is unsupported by any recognizable frame of reference, it can only become enfeebled and self-destructive."[2] Problematically, suburban and open Texas landscapes share a loose fluidity in which "horizontal flow, the horizontal organization of movement is preferred."[3] In Dallas, extreme suburban blandness and the flat open landscape make evident a lack of traditional urban topographical structure that would ordinarily provide a frame of reference.

How can students of architecture learn to position new works in this context such that their interventions will neither stand in aggressive contrast to, nor disappear into, the given, but participate with it?

Traditional city fabric provides a patchwork structure into which new works can be inserted. Without such a framework, sculptural forms are left floating in their parking lots. One possible approach to positioning architecture in such a context—the enunciation of hidden landscape orders— is revealed in Judd's precise and spare negotiation between body, land and sky.

Terrain: Landscape in Architectural Education

Landscape thinking, already valued within urban landscape practice, has become a method through which I teach architecture. Students produce work that settles between fields: landscape orders within urban settings, into which architecture is positioned.[4] Last year, in a collaborative architecture/landscape-architecture studio at the University of Texas at Arlington, we explored the potential of applying "landscape thinking"—or, more accurately, a diagrammatic thinking developed from landscape theory—to larger urban landscapes, along the way struggling to use GIS as a generative mapping tool. The work was specific to a site in Sao Paulo, Brazil,[5] with its particular social and ecological challenges.

In this essay, I discuss some of the potentials I find in using a deep physical and cultural understanding of contemporary landscape and landscape theory as a strategic framework for the teaching and practice of urban and architectural design. I illustrate these observations with studio projects in which a landscape approach repositioned student thinking about site and architecture.

I propose that a landscape approach to architecture has three main effects. The first is the implicit integration into the work of concerns relevant and important to contemporary urban design

practice in its ambitions to revitalize the city. These include ecology and sustainability, time and change both as factors and as design tools, and the large-scale site with local cultural specificities. Such concerns, I propose, are not at all unique to a landscape teaching methodology, merely harder to avoid in that context. Second, working with a physical landscape necessitates working with maps and engaging with both the potentials and the pitfalls of contemporary mapping methodologies. Here, I refer not only to notational devices for recording topography and time, but to diagrammatic or machinic mapping techniques that reveal and inspire both physical and conceptual content. Aware of the complex conversations that develop around the use of diagrammatic processes, I limit my description to areas of possibility opened up. Third, the physical and perceptual scaling of landscape—that is, of its flexible yet iterative orders—which I discern in Judd's work at Marfa, may emerge from the creative processes, revealing specific rhythms and character. While aware of the tenuousness of the idea of hidden truths within the landscape, I propose that new orderings of place can emerge, for designers, through the investigative struggle, allowing the designer to come to a specific understanding of place, to cultivate a personal site.

1. Grafts: Concerns Appropriated from Landscape

"the emphasis on temporality and transformation [...] comes in part from landscape design, which has long understood its medium— nature—to be simultaneously dynamic and systemic, and open to interventions that alter the entire system" [6]

Spatiality of Time:
The rate at which cities change has increased, and our experience of such change is exaggerated by the pace of life within them. Urban planning always provided a framework for growth, but contemporary plans must celebrate it, with change as an inevitable characteristic. Landscape embodies change. Hence, once described as landscape, it is harder for student projects to be static; plant growth, seasonal change, and fluid uses of infra-

structure lead instances into continuities. Calling work landscape is thus partly expedient: it brings issues to the table. Furthermore, landscape works, both drawn and described, articulate changes. Design is not a narrative of static frames viewed over time, but a single diagrammatic function, in which the specificity of each moment can lead to a new, unexpected result.

Large, urban projects need to respond to change, but so do small-scale ones. Corporate "hotel-ling," for example, allows no fixed desks. Yet, how can house and city, the loci of our worlds, provide anchors without turning into straight-jackets? Landscape provides three paradigms. First, the calm continuity of environmental change, in daily, seasonal and geological continuum, provides a model for flow without event. Second, landscape reads functions and motions as integral to the character of place: flows of a site, movements of water, industrial processes, even construction, become design factors, with process itself as a building block. Third, we can take advantage of the re-appearance of landscape in the cultural sphere. We learn to recognize political process, memory, and local cultural changes as inevitably marked in every landscape, and, through landscape processes, we integrate such fluctuations into the complexity of the mediated object. Again, cultural flows do not engage the reading of site but re-situate themselves as active tools of place-making. James Corner notes the shift from "landscape as a product of culture to landscape as an agent for producing and enriching culture."[7] In taking on this potential, students discover that change, negotiation, and politics are the stuff from which architecture is made, not obstacles to it.

Integral Sustainability:

Ecological sustainability must be integrated into contemporary cities. If treated as an isolated, quasi-scientific specialization, sustainability leads to simplistic responses through rigid solutions to mechanical problems. In a landscape approach, the ecology of site participates in the full conversation. Student proposals should not be isolated machines for ameliorating climatic problems, but part of a number of situated flows: continuous motions of sun and shadow, water, wind, collection and conservation, weather and decay. These and other flows constitute the panoply of networks lay-

ered over a site. Such a model provides a framework for discussion into which we can fold not only geographical networks but local ones as well: vehicular, pedestrian, and social. As a teaching tool, the landscape approach allows radical and vital political issues to be spatialized. As a design tool, it invites integrated thinking with diverse themes in layered juxtaposition.

Landscape ecology ties abstract investigation to local material specificity. Materials and their resistances are powerful teaching tools: their tangible frictions orchestrate a struggle through which design can emerge. Landscape thinking provides a critical framework for such efforts, a structured field for invention.

Specificity of Place:

Even critics of nostalgic post-modern responses to contemporary placeless-ness still search for ways to conjure up locale. Landscape practices allow particularities of place to emerge, gently and without symbolic frames. Although it has no more primary claim to regional identity than architecture, landscape may be harder to disassociate from local specificity, and may participate more easily in an evolving cultural milieu.

2. Germinations: Mapping Techniques from Landscape

"extremely opaque, imaginative, operational instruments…mappings are neither depictions nor representations, but mental constructs, ideas that enable and effect change."[8]

The physical techniques of mapping are not, themselves, neutral. Working within landscape practice, one opens teaching procedures to a range of mapping possibilities with a number of dangers and limits. Clearly, the primary benefit of the map as a notational device is that, through its abstraction, it opens representation to time. Mapping becomes the diagramming not just of data but also of processes, with the potential to reveal patterns of use and also patterns of change. The articulation of this gait or function, in the mathematical sense of that term, is a powerful contribution of landscape methodologies to architectural practices. Like musical notation, however, the map is

designed to be experienced through its effects. Here, a certain danger becomes apparent. As already necessarily a visual image, the notation of the mapping itself has a tendency to look like form. Suddenly, the mapping can slide from practice to object: a fixed, idealized, representation. The problem is obvious: imagine if music were suddenly defined as the figure of its notation.

The Generative Diagram

"Proceeding with halting steps through serial obsessions with form, language and representation–though, as will be seen, equally with program, force and performance - the diagram has seemingly emerged as the final tool for architectural production and discourse." [9]

Creativity in architecture is a complex topic. We find it hard to discuss invention, even in schools ostensibly dedicated to its cultivation. We tend to teach criticism and leave invention to emerge, anxiously. The visible architectural-idea-diagram (*e.g.*, the "parti-diagram" of the 1980s) structured architectural ambition around deeply-embedded classical positions: consistency ostensibly led to clarity, and clarity—like order and balance—was considered good. Questioning such fixities, academic use of the diagram eventually changed, taking on new roles: first, as a technique to encourage production; second, as a quasi-scientific, apparently rigorous stage of "site research" before project design; and, third, as a generator of form. R. E. Somol describes a shift in the creative role of diagrams from post-war examples (Rowe/Alexander), which attempted to represent a static truth condition, to more recent uses (Eisenman/Koolhaas) as a method of actively projecting repetition through divergent series.

Landscape mapping in this context can be investigated for its potential to act generatively, as a diagram. This may be both its most powerful and its most problematic role. As a creative tool, mapping ambitiously sponsors the unfolding of imaginative desires and possibilities, what James Corner calls "a theatre of operations." Certainly, strategic mapping practices, such as those discussed above, foster investigation of site with far reaching potential, provoking creative thinking.

However, I differentiate that from the inspirational, "diagrammatic" role of mapping, described by Deleuze as "a catastrophe happening unexpectedly to the canvas, inside figurative or probabilistic data."[10] Deleuze himself made this distinction clear in his assertion that "the diagram is a possibility of fact—it is not the fact itself."[11] This "chaos…but also a seed of order" evolves via a figure or technique isolated, momentarily, from place or meaning, providing a catalyst for imaginative play. In this context, we can join Somol in describing diagrammatic work as projective in that it opens new—or, more accurately, virtual—territories for practice.[12] But teaching must not be tied to specific operational techniques of mapping or folding; these techniques cannot be fixed without losing the very anti-empirical position they attempt to reach. Furthermore, such practices must still struggle to "negotiate the gap between the diagram and the material event."[13]

3. Conclusion: The Fears of Landscape

As creative tools, methodologies of landscape mapping are typically haunted by at least two fears: that nothing vital of the original map will be preserved in the work and that an anticipated yet hidden truth may not be discovered. They are also often burdened by a secret anxiety that the methodology was just a "getting going," irrelevant to the project itself. Those fears are grounded in the idea of isolated stages in a design process, with landscape mapping as a research phase and a wide, difficult gap between that and the design phase. However, if we define the landscape itself as our discourse, then both mappings and design proposals can be seen as continuous, iterative stages of the same work. The gap need not be bridged, because it no longer exists. A search for such continuity can be recognized, for example, in emerging work at the Architectural Association, London, in which active mapping practices participate in a strategic process "of systemic idealization and breeding over time…[the work] is not preconceived as an ideal but generated as a potential."[14] Thus, the mapped work is temporarily articulated in both architectural practice and

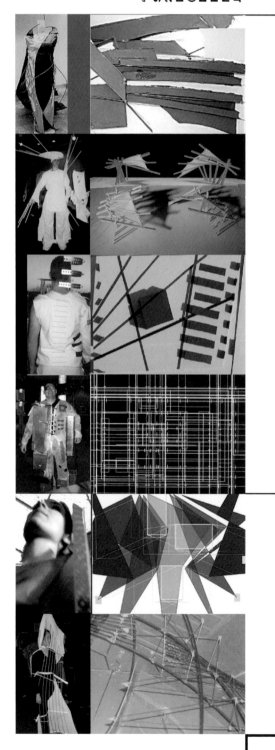

"Inhabited Illusions: a Study of Skins," UTA, 2002. Body as site, Landscape as site. (Kristen, Stuart, Randall, David, Amy, Alejandro, Paula, Jazeel, Victoria, Mackenzie, Elizabeth, José Luis)

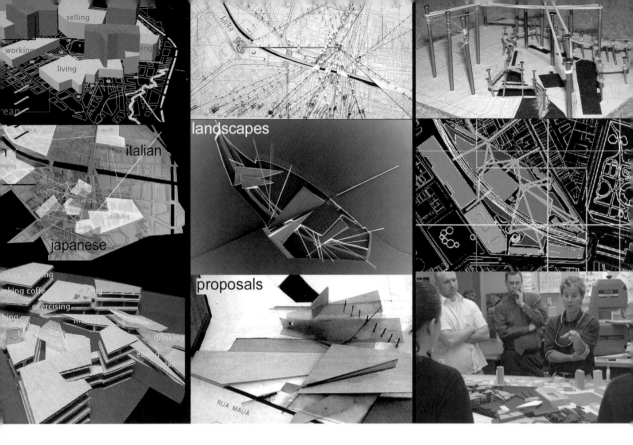

landscape discourse: it is never completed.

In Texas, my architecture students try to design landscape. Patterns are discovered and created, emerging from hidden orders of the full environment: topographies, infrastructures, ecologies, histories, even memories and perceptual knowings of site, perhaps invisible but certainly real. These patterns constitute a net—neither geometric, nor historic, but a fabric generated from the land. The design of this fabric is the primary topic of the studio. Into its order, a building project is placed, carefully designed and detailed with the architectural tools at our disposal: material, program, change. The building might be drawn alone but will be the first of an unending sequence, hinting at its continuity, just as the first few steps can hint at the order of a dance. Like Judd's boxes, it will change the pace of the walker and his or her view of the horizon, both revealing the existing landscape and altering our confidence and pace in the experience of it.

Jessie Marshall, *Dip. Arch. (RIBA), is a practicing architect and a Lecturer in the School of Architecture, University of Texas at Arlington. She is also a doctoral candidate at the Architectural Association, London.*

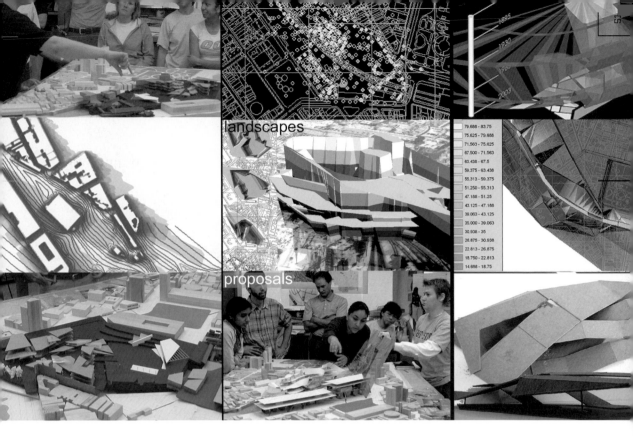

landscapes

proposals

Sao Paulo Project, UTA, Spring 2003.

NOTES

1 _ Colin Rowe and Fred Koetter, *Collage City* (Cambridge, MA: The MIT Press, 1978), 64.

2 _ Ibid.

3 _ J. B. Jackson, "The Love of Horizontal Spaces," *Discovering the Vernacular Landscape* (New Haven, CT: Yale University Press, 1984), 70.

4 _ Recently at University of Texas, Arlington, and previously at Cambridge, UK, and Chinese University, Hong Kong.

5 _ Working with Carlos Leite, Mackenzie University, Sao Paulo, Brazil.

6 _ Detlef Mertins, "landscapeurbanismhappensintime," in *Landscape Urbanism* (London: Architectural Association, 2003), 135.

7 _ James Corner, "Introduction," *Recovering Landscape* (New York, NY: Princeton Architectural Press, 1999), 4.

8 _ James Corner, "The Agency of Mapping," *Mappings*, ed. Denis Cosgrove (London: Reaktion Press, 1999), 250.

9 _ Robert Somol, "Dummy Text, or the Diagrammatic Basis of Contemporary Architecture," in Peter Eisenman, *Diagram Diaries* (New York, NY: Universe Books/ Rizzoli, 1999), 7.

10 _ Gilles Deleuze, "The Diagram," *The Deleuze Reader*, ed. Constantin Boundas (New York, NY: Columbia University Press, 1993), 194.

11 _ Ibid., 199

12 _ Somol, "Dummy Text," 24.

13 _ Andrew Benjamin, AA Lecture Series, 2004.

14 _ Ciro Najle, "Plan," in *Landscape Urbanism* (London: Architectural Association, 2003), 119. The work described at the AA takes place in Najle's Landscape Urbanism studio, which is illustrated in the book.

Hydraulic Canal Greenway
Jana Kasikova

This proposal consists of a comprehensive park system for the city of Niagara Falls that would connect the Reservation at the Falls to the rest of the city. The greenway would open the city to all the visitors as well as provide green-space for its residents. The greenway would follow along the past flow of the waters that were contained in the Hydraulic Canal that can, again, serve as a connector through the city. The original route of the canal would be reinforced by two rows of trees throughout. Special design features will mark four locations: the High Banks, two blocks between Main Street and Niagara Street, the block between Falls Street and Rainbow Boulevard along the John B. Day Boulevard, and Port Day. At those locations, the canal will be uncovered. The dirt from the excavation will be used to create a mound that will than mark the pressure tunnel (100 feet below the surface). The former location of the old bridges will be marked by a change of pavement. The old rail yards will also be referenced through the creation of a series of long narrow gardens. Some of the original streets at the sites will be reinstituted to create connecting pedestrian walkways, and parking will be redesigned.

MAIN STREET

1ST STREET

2ND STREET

ARCHITECTURE AND LANDSCAPE: MAKING AND UNMAKING THE WORLD

Lynda Schneekloth

Architecture and landscape architecture, intimate and inseparable both in the world and within the realm of ideas, historically shared a common practice. Modernity's obsession with professionalism and boundary-making divided the two disciplines/ professions into separate, though related, practices and educational structures. Many are beginning to see through that division.[1] Boundary blurring is occurring in diverse ways, such as the recent publications that bring the two disciplines together, and also pedagogically by having a landscape architect on an architecture faculty, a position that I hold at the Department of Architecture, University at Buffalo.[2]

Landscape theory, teaching, and practice in many ways reinforce architectural education, and yet, the focus that places work on the earth and in the world opens interesting pedagogical opportunities. The dominant theoretical and practical aspects of architecture encourage students to concentrate on the objects of their making; exposure to landscape, as I have employed it in studio and seminars, attempts to widen that focus and extend each student's field of concern.

The concept of place is a powerful theoretical structure for teaching landscape in architecture studios and other classes. It has replaced "site" in my pedagogy, even though recent scholarship on site has outlined a more inclusive way of implacing architecture in the contexts of location, meaning,

The Working Landscape: Land Use Reversal

Brett Gawronski

The idea behind this proposal is to reverse what power and industry have done to the land, by reversing the system of taking water from the Niagara River; rather, water is purified after use on the site of the old Power Plant. Phyto-remediation is used to clean the water, diverted from the existing water treatment plant and returned back to the upper river. The new plant beds mark the sites of the now-gone powerhouse structures. The volume of the two former power generation buildings is marked by a steel framing system covered by vegetation. Other aspects of the project include the Transformer house being turned into a Historical museum, the Tesla statue as well as the powerhouse entrance being moved from Goat Island to its original location, and the repositioning of the historical portage house fireplace also to its original location.

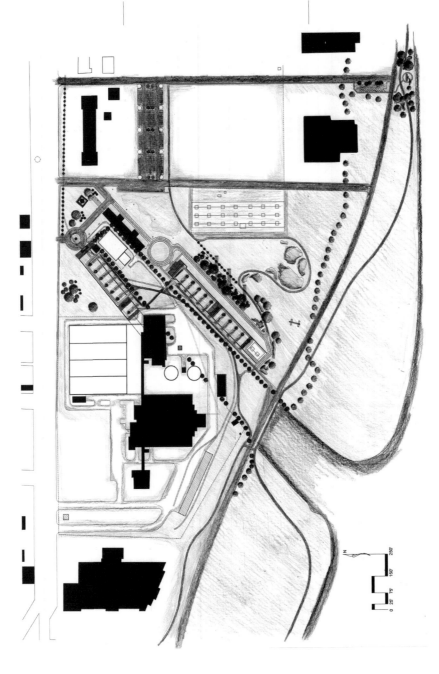

activities, and concepts.[3] Yet, *place*, the more ancient word, brings back architecture's relationships to specific locales and cultures. Today's post-empirical students are highly resistant to technical rational approaches such as site analysis. More poetical discussions of place inquiry, as outlined by Christophe Girot in his essay, "Four Trace Concepts in Landscape Architecture," enable students to understand genuine connections to both site and program, as exemplified in designs and research projects alike.[4]

A subject rarely discussed in architecture but obvious in landscape is the extent of the unmaking of the world that occurs with every design intervention. This shadow side of architecture, discussed in my seminars and studios, creates disorder in the world in some places so that order is created in others. Unmaking is a part of making and, if considered as such, the preservation of the land and our existing built fabric take on a deeper meaning, layering both the ethical and practical discourses of sustainability. The cost to the world of each making is part of the pedagogy of the Waste Studio I have taught at Buffalo. We explore waste places, such as the toxic waste site at Love Canal, and the waste of things that occurs in the production and transportation of even common materials such as dry wall and glass.

Studio projects focused on public history have been particularly successful in engaging architecture students in landscape, since the critical connections between place, history, stories and programs are rich for design exploration and capture their imagination. Coupled with Girot's "landing, grounding, finding, and founding" activities of place inquiry, landscape design is experienced as embedded in a project rather than constraining it; the work is recognized as respectful of historic structure—revealing them without manipulating them. For example, my studio on the Buffalo Grain Elevators required the students to address the field within which these elevators reside rather than changing or manipulating the elevators themselves; in another studio, the story of hydropower in Niagara Falls focused on connecting the various power plants, including ruins, into a connective tissue that united the Niagara River to the city and to traces and remnants of a former canal.

Architecture students typically both know and don't know about landscape design in that they do have general design skills but are unfamiliar with the scale, structure, constraints, materials, and representations of outdoor space. Confirming their knowledge is an important step. Yet it is also critical for them to know the limits of their knowledge and how other discourses address some of the issues in a different or more comprehensive way. Natural processes, for example, are engaged in architecture. However, their effects on buildings are slow, hardly noticeable, and rarely considered;

in fact, architecture usually attempts to hold time and arrest these effects. Landscape design is dependent on a creative deployment of natural processes: daily, seasonal, yearly, with fluid cycles of birth and death. At some point, difference in degree becomes difference in kind.

One of my most successful pedagogical activities has been the incorporation of on-going charettes in landscape studios. We discuss different types of landscape representation in a series of drawing exercises, since the softness of the landscape does not lend itself to many of the architecture students' existing computer or hand-drawing techniques. Other issues of representation include the use of vegetation as other-than-architectural elements, often rendered as inappropriately scaled pompoms on sticks. Students learn the formal properties of different types of vegetation and how to represent them: heights and widths, branching patterns, textures, and seasonal conditions. The articulation of these patterns becomes part of their conscious decision making. I do not teach them the names of plants and trees; I focus instead on their ability to make formal, performance, and ecological specifications and urge them to be in touch with a landscape architect or other professional for the most appropriate species to use. This is my attempt to help eradicate the phenomenon of architects specifying only one or two trees out of a diverse universe because they happen to know their names, while enabling students to form a different relationship with the vegetative world on which our lives depend.

Landscape principles are introduced to teach the perceptual differences in the reading of indoor and outdoor space: abstract and bodily measurement of known outdoor spaces such as the quad they walk through everyday are compared to known indoor rooms. Formal design strategies are explored through in-class charettes on specific landscape styles, such as classical traditions or modern landscape designs. In those charettes, students are required to use a style to design a space with which they are already familiar, with an immediate crit and discussion after. Because style is used more freely in landscape design, students develop a wide range of strategies from which to draw—something less available in architecture, according to their reading of their own education.

Making plans in landscape is another struggle for many architecture students, since there is no such thing as white space. They have to assume responsibility for every inch of their plans, forcing them to see the ground as a continuous plane even while learning to design with layers of vegetation on a single drawing. The students report that this is both frustrating and liberating; it forces a discipline but also gives them the sense of mastery over concept and design development.

Experiencing Schoellkopf
Julie Cannon

How does one integrate the old with the new without interfering with its historical significance? In order to leave the ruins of the Schoellkopf Plant as they are, the proposal creates a number of access structures, such as a glass elevator and pathways that are significantly different and use modern materials in order to distinguish between the old and the new. The use of different materials also translates into the interpretive aspects of the project. Steel frames are used to outline exterior walls of power stations that once stood on the site to communicate a sense of volume and scale. Also, a series of comparative images are provided along the trail to tell the story of the Schoellkopf site.

I have constructed a graduate seminar on the vernacular landscape in which we look relentlessly at the everyday world—malls and vacant lots, highways, main streets, and industrial wastelands. Architecture often focuses on the gems and the uniquely designed places, whereas most of the modern landscape is, in fact, a sea of distressed and, frankly, ugly spaces. As Robert Sardello wrote, "the world's body has entered a state of almost irretrievable numbness. No healing will be found for this illness that will not entail a reversal of our way of imagining the world . . ."[5] As designers, we need to find ways to listen to the world and speak its language if we are to engage the disturbed and disconnected places of late modernity.

One of the exercises in the graduate seminar is a project called Under the Bridge, in which students read and re-present a space that is left over from other design decisions, such as highway construction. Before jumping into fixing it, they are asked to give the space a voice metaphorically, to confront its origin and its condition with a sympathetic, rather than disregarding, standpoint. Only after that engagement are they asked to respond to the place. Projects over the years have ranged from traditional beautifications, to artistic proposals that reveal distressed aspects of the place by rendering them visible to others, to actual interventions on the sites.

An unflinching exploration of the origin, development, and current condition of the landscape the students have always known and take for granted as the invisible field of their lives facilitates their engagement in architecture as placemaking. Students recognize that designers do not create bad or ugly places intentionally; nevertheless, our lives are filled with them, in part because of the consequences of design decisions. An aim of this landscape pedagogy is to enable students to see that the existing geography of anywhere is not inevitable and that they have the insight to see through the pain of the place-resistant world they have inherited—a critical lesson for anyone who will become an unmaker and maker of the world.

Lynda H. Schneekloth, *ASLA, is a Professor at the School of Architecture and Planning at the University at Buffalo, SUNY. Her teaching, scholarship and practice focus on placemaking and the interface between landscape and architecture, between the earth and our makings. Schneekloth lives by the mighty Niagara River, and much of her work centers on the place of that river in the history, ecology, construction and future of the bi-national region. She recently co-edited a theme issue for the* Journal of Architectural Education *(57/3) on "Landscape and Architecture." In addition to many articles, she is author, with Robert Shibley, of* Placemaking: The Art and Practice of Building Communities; *Ordering Space: Types in Architecture and Design, with Karen Franck; and* Changing Places: Re-Making Institutional Buildings, *with Marcia Feuerstein and Barbara Campagna.*

the Architecture Department offers an "Area of Concentration" in Landscape and Sustainability that enables students to focus in the field. Furthermore, we have faculty interested in issues of landscape. Professors of architecture, including the late Professor Michael Brill, and Professors Bonnie Ott, Ian Taberner, and Gary Day, have won landscape design competitions. As part of the Area of Concentration, we have developed a summer abroad program "Sustainable Futures" in Costa Rica in collaboration with landscape and planning schools.

3 _ Carol Burns, "On Site: Architectural Preoccupations," in Andrea Kahn, ed., *Drawing, Building, Text* (New York, NY: Princeton Architectural Press, 1991), 141-167; David Leatherbarrow, *Uncommon Ground: Architecture, Technology, and Topography*, (Cambridge, MA: The MIT Press, 2000).

4 _ Christophe Girot, "Four Trace Concepts in Landscape Architecture," in James Corner, ed., *Recovering Landscape: Essays in Contemporary Landscape Architecture* (New York, NY: Princeton Architectural Press, 1999).

5 _ Robert Sardello, "House and City," *Facing the World with Soul* (Hudson, NY: Lindisfarne Press, 1992), 34. Among other texts used in the seminar are James Hillman, "Anima Mundi: The Return of the Soul to the World," *Spring* (Dallas, TX: 1982); Michael Sorkin, ed., *Variations on a Theme Park* (New York, NY: Hill and Wang, 1992); and Michael Soule and Gary Lease, *Reinventing Nature?* (Washington, DC: Island Press, 1995).

NOTES

1 _ See, especially, Anita Berrizbeitia and Linda Pollak, *Inside Outside: between architecture and landscape* (Gloucester, MA: Rockport, 1999); Jan Birksted, ed., *Relating Architecture to Landscape* (New York, NY: E and FN SPON, 1999); James Corner, ed., *Recovering Landscape* (New York, NY: Princeton Architectural Press, 1999); Keller Easterling, *Organization Space: Landscapes, Highways, and Houses in America* (Cambridge, MA: The MIT Press, 1999).

2 _ The University of Buffalo does not have a landscape department, but

THE SPACE IN-BETWEEN

Susan Conger-Austin

Observing interactions between the built and natural environments provides deeper understanding of a place over time. Locally inflected, the tactile features of landscape include topography, ecozone, climate, and natural light, offering the wonder and excitement of continual change. Typically, we are too busy or preoccupied to notice those changes. It is through the integration of architecture and landscape architecture that one begins to see differently, to slow down and observe the intimate qualities of a specific place over time.

Over the past five years of studio teaching at the Illinois Institute of Technology, I have found that introducing architectural problems that blur buildings and nature helps to highlight important issues in creating meaningful spaces/places. This was especially true in the studio project I assigned in Spring 2003. Entitled "The Space In-Between," the project was a "Leisure Collective" for the University of Chicago Graduate School of Business. The program included a health club, juice bar, pub, small movie theatre for art films, individual reading rooms, and outdoor space. To underscore the importance of intertwining outside and inside, I team taught with a landscape architect, Chandra Goldsmith.

The intent of the studio was to create a space linking two separate and stylistically distinct buildings on the campus of the University of

diagrams and building analysis

uses   connections   light

—— topography
•••••••• architectural elements
glass roof / furniture

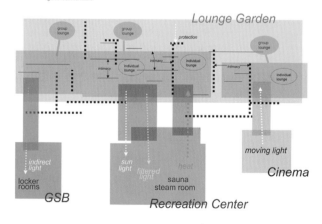

Figure 6

Chicago—a brand new Rafael Vinoly—designed buisness school and a limestone gothic student center—through careful study and understanding of site, program, and vision. Creating spaces and structures of greater intimacy, intricacy, and connectivity was critical to retaining the sense of scale and complexity that characterize the University of Chicago campus. Currently, all of the new buildings and projects proposed for the campus are freestanding, contrary to the historic tradition of the University's quadrangles with their tight proximity and numerous connections between buildings. If an institution such as the University of Chicago is not only to survive but to flourish in contemporary society, it must be forward thinking in its physical as well as its intellectual expression. However, it also must not lose sight of its past. Through the "Leisure Collective" project, students had the opportunity to create an architecture that blurred the distinctions between open and enclosed space, the built and the natural, the creative and the contextual.

One of the outcomes of "The Space In-Between" was that students were no longer working in isolation on a specific site. Instead, in combining architectural analyses with landscape design, students were compelled to investigate both the immediate surroundings as well as the campus as a whole **[Figs. 3 & 4]**. That extensive research of a broader area, rather than of a specific site, revealed a number of issues that were not readily apparent at first glance. For example, questions regarding the scale and complexity of the project were raised, and solutions were expressed through a series of diagrams focusing on connection and light within the specified site boundaries **[Figs. 5]**. Through the repeated gestures of patterns in those diagrams, meaning was found in the intertwining of the built form with the landscape. Relations between light and shadow, color and texture, solid and void, order and disorder were revealed and expressed by this analysis, leading to more complex yet intimate spaces. In addition, time-specific analysis—in terms of hours as well as seasons—became a critical factor in understanding the site. Frequent visits over the course of the semester revealed patterns of light and shadow, circulation systems, and cycles of plant growth. The final project translated those issues and corresponding diagrams into a three-dimensional landscape expanding the traditional notion of what constitutes an architectural project **[Figs. 1-2, & 6]**.

An architectural design studio with a strong landscape component can support a broader range of solutions and didactic experiences. Integrating the pedagogies of architecture and landscape architecture enhances students' perceptions of how the relationship of outdoor space to the built environment can relay specific messages about culture, people, and place. In the confluence of the two disciplines, students learn to see things differently and, in so doing, renewed energy and awareness of our surroundings are made possible.

Susan Conger-Austin, *M.Arch., is an Assistant Professor and Director of the Professional Masters Programs in the College of Architecture at Illinois Institute of Technology. She is also the founder of the firm S. Conger Architects, LLC.*

LAND

AMÉNAGEMENT

IN THE

PEDAGOGY OF

_ARCHITECTURAL DESIGN

Figure 1. Analog diagram. (Chang; Arch 703; 2000)[i]

donna luckey

During my graduate studies in the University of Califronia–Berkeley architecture program, Christopher Alexander asked me, "What do you care about the most?" and I answered simply, "the land." I realized then that I wanted to shift my academic focus, taking the rigorous approach of "design theory and methods" with me as I explored what it meant, as an architect, to have such passion for the land. How could I combine my head and my heart? That was when I first encountered Ralph Borsordi's concept of "trusterty," an alternative view of real estate or "property," which was a key point in the early land trust movements in the United States.[1] Subsequently, in my Ph.D. qualifying exam essays at Berkeley, I defended the idea of "trusterty" and described how it complemented Aldo Leopold's influential land ethic.[2] In addition to ongoing studies of Native American philosophies and new explorations of deep ecology, I read about sustainable systems. In the 1970s, the term "sustainable" was applied mainly to yields in fisheries, agriculture, and even northern California forestry, as exemplified by the Pacific Lumber Company practices of that time.

During those intense years of study in California, I found opportunities to test my ideas while working at the State Coastal Conservancy (SCC) in Oakland. That agency was originally conceived in the 1976 California Coastal Plan as something akin to a land trust for resource

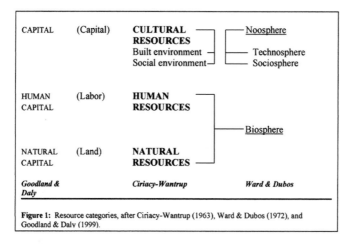

Figure 1: Resource categories, after Ciriacy-Wantrup (1963), Ward & Dubos (1972), and Goodland & Daly (1999).

protection in the coastal zone.[3] In its formative years, we described the SCC as a hybrid of an urban redevelopment company and the Trust for Public Lands. My dissertation on alternative land relationships was informed by, and emerged out of, my four years of experience at the SCC. I had learned how land and resource protection—indeed, how any planning—must be a political and participatory process, not just a passion emerging from a philosophical point of view.

Among various challenges to my dissertation work, my mentor, Horst Rittel, rejected the term "sustainable" as too controversial. (Remember, this is the late 1970s!) That led me to seek an alternative and to discover the incredibly rich French term *aménagement*, with its origin in fourteenth-century Swiss forestry.[4] The Swiss *aménagiste* was planter, gardener, thinner, cultivator, logger, and miller of the trees in his forest. I adapted the term to *land aménagement*, defining the new expression as the ongoing *process* of planning, design, implementation, and stewardship.[5] As architects and planners, we cannot simply develop an idea and set it adrift. Instead, we must follow each project beyond its initial implementation, through lifelong stewardship. Land and its resources are given to us in trust by those who will inherit them from us, and we must en*liven* our world in all ways possible while these resources are in our stewardship. A celebrated Kenyan

saying reflects this idea: "Let us look at the world as something we have not inherited from our parents but borrowed from our children."[6]

In the fall of 1983, I began teaching architectural design studios in the School of Architecture and Urban Design at the University of Kansas, Lawrence. I have developed many courses during the subsequent years to bring an appreciation of land and its resources to architecture and planning students. I continue to protect land resources through the Kansas Land Trust, serving on the Board of Directors since 1991, one year after its founding. I believe that the range and orientation of my experience, and the depth and rigor of my explorations of land, have given me a useful, interdisciplinary approach to teaching and other work. This is exemplified in a model, which I developed as a teaching tool, and that outlines resources and defines land within the context of conservation economics. **[Fig. 2]**

This model began as a way to represent Siegfried von Ciriacy-Wantrup's definitions of resources and has evolved to show parallel definitions up through the current usage of "natural" and "human capital."[7] The model provides one framework through which architecture students can understand and evaluate their world. It also parallels Ian McHarg's influential map overlay structure, which he introduced in 1969 as a way to "design with nature."[8] That system of analysis, which McHarg imported to design and planning from geography, identifies variables specifically as natural or cultural resources. Both of our models clarify the relationships between the built environment (cultural resources), human design decisions, and natural systems (natural resources). Using these models as a starting point, I provide my students with several additional ways to explore the relationship of the land to their design work.

One of these is an assignment to develop checklists of questions, which the students then use to evaluate regional design and landscape projects during site visits. The lessons from these visits are then tied to an essay of reflection concerning each student's final design project for the semester. Examples from the checklists show the range of variables the students consider when analyzing the ties between buildings and the land.

Natural Resources

• How does the building relate to the site? Is there a better site that suits this building?
• Were there tremendous amounts of cut and fill?
• Was wildlife impacted? Negative? Positive?
• How is runoff treated? Is it retained on site or directed to infrastructure?
• Were water systems (*e.g.*, lakes, rivers, streams, underground water) conserved?

Cultural Resources

• How does the building relate to the surrounding sites? Buildings? Contexts?
• Do the building materials have a high or low embodied energy?
• What are the social/economical benefits to the community and context (or lack of)?
• Does the building educate the community about green architecture?

Also, some idiosyncratic questions that address perspective and scale:

• Can a rhinoceros graze there?
• How do you find a lost contact lens?
• How does this project relate to systemic shifts in the universe?

Teaching graduate design studio is, for me, a welcome challenge. In my approach, the question, "How can we build on the knowledge and experience brought by the diverse backgrounds of the students?" is just as critical as "How can I integrate landscape, site, and environmental planning issues into studio projects?" One key objective is to intertwine bioregionalism and an appreciation of the land into the design consciousness of each student: How will land be a critical part of design, woven into their experience from this semester

onward? In addition to site visits and semester-long reflections on the issues described above, I assign design projects that focus specifically on landscape. In introducing the semester, I ask each student to define a "place in the landscape" as a way to learn how each participant responds to the land through the design, as well as to learn about our local Kansas bioregion. This project reveals each student's own understanding of place, with its *unique* story and design resolution.

A key project in my graduate studio is to design a co-housing community that uses sustainability as its model for human, cultural, and natural resources **[Fig. 2]**. Working in groups, students address the land in many different ways as each project evolves. For example, an especially strong project, developed in Fall 2000, reflected the diverse backgrounds of the students as well as their participatory planning and creative process. The early individual design proposals included analog models for space and community as introduced by a student from China with an economics background. His figure-ground analyses evolved from the traditional use for representing built form and open areas to a representation in plan and section of a high density proposal. In the final iteration, these analogs represented the actual dwellers of the co-housing community, in which members would shift forward into leadership roles according to their different skills and recede when needing privacy or retiring for a period. The student's powerful use of analog led the group to develop analog models for each of their clusters of dwelling units. **[Fig. 1]**

This group also engaged an evolved understanding of *bioregion* and landscape. Their project started at a bank of the Kansas, or Kaw, River, but the individual designs very quickly moved out into the river itself. The final iterations of their collective design demonstrated an understanding of the Kaw watershed which recognized multiple factors: *waterscape* as part of our landscape; the historic importance of the Kaw River to the development of both Lawrence and their site; the human, cultural, and natural resource implications of bridging the Kaw with their project; and how a future, sustainable co-housing community would incorporate the river in as many ways as possible. Their understanding of *aménagement* was clear in the cycles of daily, seasonal, and annual rituals tied to the community's habitation of a place of the river.

The choices of sites for the co-housing project often include those determined through an earlier map overlay process. Using basic tutorials, I also introduce Geographic Information Systems (GIS) as a tool for designers, relating GIS to the McHargian site analyses already undertaken. In Spring 2004, I added a GIS component that described the site for our final design project—

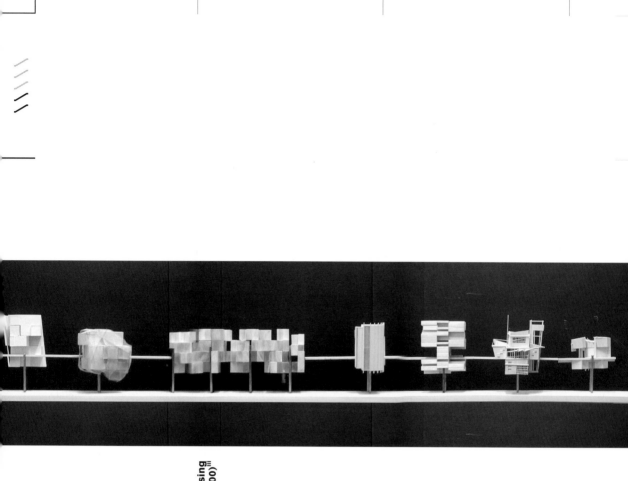

Figure 3. Final iteration of bridging co-housing project. (Arch 703; 2000)[iii]

a Waldorf School. As with other programs given for the final project of the semester (such as: an environmental education center, a botanical garden and arboretum, a vineyard and winery complex), the Waldorf School project required each student to develop a specific philosophical position regarding land and environment that goes beyond traditional site planning and landscape design. The integration of site and natural systems into the education of students in the Waldorf School program parallels the integration into studio education of these same aspects of our landscape.

To the extent that we are all members of a bioregional community, I want students to recognize the role that their specific home landscapes play in their design heritage. We look at bioregions from different perspectives—as watersheds, as vernacular landscapes, as home communities. I believe that a holistic, systems-based understanding of natural, cultural, and human resources is necessary to move into a sustainable future. The *aménagement* of our land—and of our architecture—depends upon it.

donna luckey, M.Arch., Ph.D., is an Associate Professor in the School of Architecture and Urban Design at the University of Kansas, Lawrence. She serves as president of the Board of Directors of the Kansas Land Trust.

NOTES

1 _ See John Blackmore, "Community trusts offer a hopeful way back to the land," *The Smithsonian* 9: 3 (June 1978): 97-109. Ralph Borsodi, along with Robert Swann, founded The Institute for Community Economics, and the land trust movement in the United States owes its origins to these two men.

2 _ Aldo Leopold, *A Sand County Almanac* (New York, NY: Oxford University Press, 1968; 1st ed., 1949).

3 _ California Coastal Commission, *The California Coastal Plan* (San Francisco: California Coastal Commission, 1976).

4 _ Émile Littré, *Dictionnaire de la langue française* (Paris: Librairie Hachette, 1874), I, 127, s.v. "aménagement."

5 _ donna luckey, "Architecture and *Aménagement*: Responsibilities in Environmental Resource Planning," *Proceedings of the 72nd Annual Meeting of the Association of Collegiate Schools of Architecture: Architecture and the Future* [March 1984] (Washington, DC: ACSA, 1984).

6 _ Ecological Design Group, *Ecolog: Courses and Resources in Appropriate Technology and Ecological Design at Berkeley* (Berkeley, CA: Ecological Design Group, University of California, 1980).

7 _ See Siegfried von Ciriacy-Wantrup, *Resource Conservation: Economics and Policies* (Berkeley, CA: University of California, Division of Agricultural Sciences, 1968).

8 _ Ian McHarg, *Design with Nature* (Garden City, NY: Doubleday Press, 1969).

i _ Richard Chang, Arch 703 (Fall 2000), School of Architecture, University of Kansas, Lawrence, semester project.

ii _ donna luckey, "Critical Design Inquiry of the Environment: Extending Experience from a Graduate Architecture Studio," in *Toward a Critical Pedagogy for the Environment: Proceedings of the 1998 ACSA West Regional Meeting*, (Berkeley, CA: Association of Collegiate Schools of Architecture, 2002): 29-1 to 29-15.

iii _ Richard Chang, Joshua Keal, Ana Paz, Nathan Rapp, Michael Russo, Ryan Worman, Billy Williams, Arch 703 (Fall 2000), School of Architecture and Urban Design, University of Kansas, Lawrence,

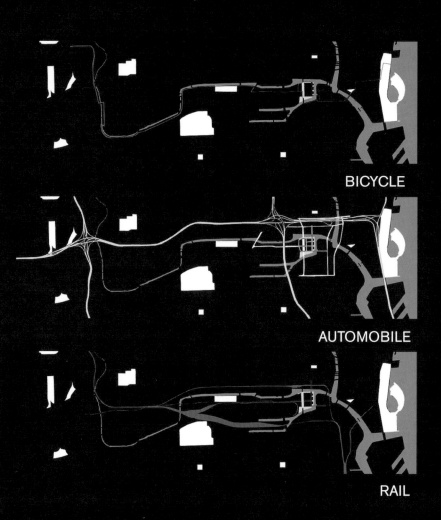

BICYCLE

AUTOMOBILE

RAIL

Figure 1: The *Path* (a walking/cycling trail) in the context of the landscape network. Designed by Robert Gamperl, Sara Schrank, and Sarah Thompson.

Ray Isaacs

THE NOT-SO-SECRET AGENDA OF A LANDSCAPE GUERILLA

"Landscape architecture!" he said emphatically. This was the response from the department chair when I asked what he wanted me to teach in the Architecture Program at the University of Wisconsin-Milwaukee. I had applied for the job because of other interests in their program. Yet, the opportunity to teach landscape architecture to architecture students—and to be given a lot of latitude as to how to go about it—was an intriguing challenge…and potentially a lot of fun! I accepted the offer. At UWM, I have since been known as "the landscape guy," though once I was introduced as "our landscape guerrilla." I have to admit, I prefer the latter. It implies a license to destroy. The agenda of a guerrilla is to overthrow the status quo, to disrupt the prevailing structure and patterns. Guerrilla tactics require a good working knowledge of the terrain and the ability to strike quickly at multiple points, but all of that within a strategy.

As a landscape guerrilla, my agenda is to shatter students' preconceived, naïve understanding of landscape architecture as something *added on* to architecture. Here's an anecdotal example. Early in my first semester, a student walked into my office, a graduate student—we'll call her Bobby. After introducing herself, Bobby came right to the point: "I'm putting together my thesis committee. My project is the renovation and reuse of a building downtown. There is a space in

Figure 2. The *Path* (the same walking/cycling trail) at the scale of sensual experience. Designed by Robert Gamperl, Sara Schrank, and Sarah Thompson.

front of the building; so, there will be some *land-scaping* involved." Yes! She had identified the right person, she thought. Need to put some trees in front of your building? Go see the landscape guy.

I said, as politely as I could, "I'm not really interested in that," but, my look probably said a lot more. I went on to say that if she were interested in rethinking aspects of her project—upon which I elaborated regarding issues of context, meaning, and so on—I would be interested. "Think about it, then come and see me again."

Bobby didn't come back. Yet, she and others since have clarified for me their conception of landscape architecture. It is *landscaping*! Landscape architecture is what you plant around your building when it is finished. Despite my colleagues emphases on landscape and context in their instruction, the general working concept among students seems to be "landscape *and* architecture" as separate realms. As they see it, architects—and architecture students—design buildings. Their task ends at the threshold… unless there is *landscaping* to be added. This concept of landscape *and* architecture is likely a notion that preceded their entry into the study of architecture. However, for reasons about which I can only speculate, the concept is reinforced in their early years of study. Perhaps in their eagerness to design buildings, they ignore broader possibilities of environmental design.

The term "*green* architecture" doesn't help matters. "*Green*," as our students see it, is the current adjective of choice to distinguish buildings designed consciously and rigorously to be natural resource friendly—in other words, ecological. Plants are also *green*—many shades of green, I frequently point out. Landscapes are *green*. Landscape architecture is *green*. It's about sustainability. The landscape guy can help us green our buildings! This level of thinking is certainly more sophisticated than *landscaping*. However, it, too, falls short. *Green* architecture usually includes only building systems. "My building will have photovoltaics, daylighting…oh, and a *green* roof." I quickly learned that the students' understanding of broader natural processes is, like many of their green roof designs, too thin to be effective. Here, too, landscape architecture is something *added-on* to the building.

Yes, natural processes are essential to landscape architecture…and social processes are as well. Plants are components of landscapes, and planting design is within the practice of landscape architecture. And buildings? They are certainly part of the landscape. I find it hard to see why building design is not encompassed within the practice of landscape architecture. To design a building is to propose a transformed landscape, to alter natural systems, to affect human experiences, to create new places, to change movement patterns and views, to add new meaning to a place. Landscape architecture is not something added to the building. The building is *embedded within* the landscape. To practice architecture is to be—wittingly or unwittingly—practicing landscape architecture. My agenda, then, is to deconstruct notions of *added-on* landscape architecture and to offer serious teaching about the making of landscapes; the ongoing forces that shape them, including architecture; and the sensual experiences that result.

With this strategy in mind—overthrowing the *landscape architecture as added on* status quo with an *architecture as embedded within landscape architecture* perspective—the specific tactics could be planned, implemented, and reconsidered. Guerrillas hit quickly on multiple fronts. With encouragement from the department chair, a teaching plan was developed, which allowed me to strike with multiple formats from different levels of the curriculum…the terrain.

The terrain is as follows. At UWM, as in most architecture programs, a core of design studios is surrounded by support courses; then, farther out on the periphery, there are several elective courses. Landscape architecture courses are on the periphery and include:

• A junior-level lecture course (383) designed for a large audience.
• A senior/graduate-level seminar (584) focused on urban landscape architecture.
• An advanced-level design studio (645) of my creation, which allows a group of students to explore designing buildings and places…*with a landscape attitude.*[1]

The courses are enjoyable to teach and feedback from the students has been very positive. A

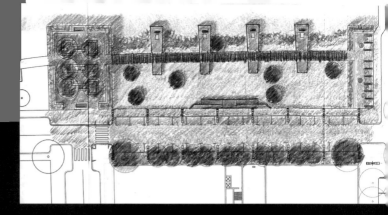

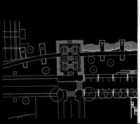

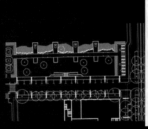

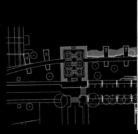

common comment is that it is refreshing to be learning something different—a different perspective on the environment, different terminology and typologies, different examples, different heroes (Olmsted instead of Wright, Halprin instead of Meier, Schwartz instead of Gehry)—from what is repeated in other courses. In response to the last essay question of the 383 final exam, a student wrote, "I now realize that landscape architecture is more than trees and tulips…" In the final document of the studio course, a student wrote, "The things I learned in this course are countless…that there are no independent projects…" She means to say that in the urban landscape all buildings and places are part of a connected network, that no building or open space stands alone. An invited critic in the final review reinforced that point by summarizing, "All the spaces mean something; they all add up to something." At least some of the students in the courses are getting the point!

While I enjoy the role of the landscape guerrilla, I sometimes feel more like a missionary. Some students have embraced the practice of landscape architecture to a high degree, a few even to the extent of pursing a graduate degree in the field. Such "conversions" are rewarding, and I'm sure the landscape gods are smiling on me. However, I realize now that the impact on the larger community of 600 students is minimal. According to my colleagues, there is a trickle-down effect as students are spreading the "landscape gospel" in their other courses, particularly the design studios. This is all encouraging, and I do enjoy moments of satisfaction in seeing an emerging understanding of landscape architecture within our architecture program. However, the limits are cause for some dissatisfaction. This has led to a critical reflection on the effectiveness of the specific tactics—the three courses—in changing the conceptions of landscape architecture within the School. Is this the best way to incorporate landscape architecture into an architecture curriculum?

Three issues need to be addressed regarding the current tactics:

• Only a limited number of students can take the courses. Given the small class size necessary for studios and seminars, as well as the fact that some students take two of the three courses, only about fifty students take any of the courses in a typical year. But there is a more restrictive limitation on the side of the students. Architecture curricula are very dense, with many required courses. With landscape architecture being taught through electives, students have to choose landscape architecture or another of many valuable electives.

• Students are being exposed to landscape architecture late in their studies. Students cannot take the landscape architecture courses until their junior year (the lecture course) or later (the seminar and studio.) By that time, they have completed many of the core requirements in architecture. Taking the elective courses as *added on* to the core requirements late in the process reinforces the separateness and added-on conception of landscape architecture. In addition, students have little time remaining to integrate and explore landscape architecture within the context of succeeding courses.

• The impact of the exposure needs to be strong and quick. With students entering any of the three courses without prior exposure to landscape architecture, each course is an introduction. The challenge is to immerse the students quickly in landscape architecture in a meaningful and memorable way. Very quickly, their preconceptions of landscape architecture need to be shattered with an unforgettable impact.

In response to these issues, new tactics are in the works. At the next opportunity, the landscape guerrilla will attack the core from the inside. Given the support I receive from my colleagues, this is not quite as subversive as it sounds. The sophomore design sequence is the gateway into upper division and professional education in architecture. All students must take those courses and do well in them to go further in the program. At that level, they do not design buildings; instead, they use design to learn about conceptual and spatial design and the associated vocabulary. By incorporating my teaching into this context, concepts of landscape architecture can be interwoven seamlessly with concepts of architecture—and this at the very formative level of design education. Students will come to terms with landscape and architecture, and *embedded-in* landscape architecture, very early.

Landscape ideas will be planted earlier and more broadly. However, the elective courses will continue. Here, the issue of impact will still need to be addressed, particularly in the design studio. Borrowing from my experience teaching in landscape architecture programs, my inclination is to emphasize the holistic landscape. In a landscape architecture curriculum, where course content builds from one semester to the next, the complexity of the holistic landscape can be managed in upper level courses. However, for architecture students in the design studio, grappling with such complexity tends to lead to superficial analyses and muddled visions. With few exceptions, that dampens the potential enthusiasm and passion for discovering something as fascinating as landscape architecture. My own model of teaching urban landscape architecture and urban design in landscape architecture programs was not adequate in an architecture program.

In addressing this issue, I am developing a new tactic: introducing *holistic complexity* through *radical simplicity*. Students are presented with *the path* as the fundamental experience of the landscape. Rather than approaching the path as an extended formal (architectural) design, the experience of time and sequence is introduced with music and the concept of the score. Current experiments in the seminar course, using specific musical works to introduce structure and improvisation, color and texture, space and atmosphere, may allow us to discuss landscapes in a language—and hopefully an attitude—that does recall architecture. Miles Davis and Michael Hedges become inspirations. Lawrence and Anna Halprin become the new heroes. Hopefully, once enchanted by the potential of *the path*, students will expand their understanding to the more complex landscape network.

The reductive and simplistic approach defies my own nature, which revels in the complexity of the holistic landscape. However, I speculate that the intensity of exploration of *the path* will ultimately yield a deeper understanding of landscapes and landscape architecture, which will, in turn, make the students better architects. That is, of course, the real agenda of the landscape guerrilla.

NOTES

1 _ Raymond Isaacs, "The Landscape Matrix: Urban Landscape Networks as Frameworks for Collage Cities," in *Proceedings of the Annual Meeting of the Association of Collegiate Schools of Architecture* (2004).

Raymond Isaacs, *M.Arch (Berkeley, 1992), MLA (Berkeley, 1993), Ph.D. (Environmental Planning/Urban Design, Berkeley 1998), is an Assistant Professor in the Department of Architecture, School of Architecture and Urban Planning, University of Wisconsin-Milwaukee.*

LANDSCAPE ARCHITECTURE WITHIN THE UNIVERSITY OF TEXAS AT AUSTIN: NOTES ON THE

In 1977, I moved from the University of Pennsylvania, where I had completed a Master of Regional Planning degree, to Washington State University, where I began my first teaching position. A proposal to rename the department topped the agenda of my very first faculty meeting. My new colleagues suggested changing the name from the Department of Horticulture to the Department of Horticulture and Landscape Architecture. The change would accompany the creation of a B.S. in Landscape Architecture. Both moves were undertaken in a quest to have the landscape architecture program accredited. In addition, two new faculty members with interests in landscape had been recruited: Ken Brooks (now at Kansas State) and me. We joined three others, pushing the size over the minimum requirements of the Landscape Architecture Accreditation Board. I was also expected to contribute to a new regional planning degree in Washington State's innovative and interdisciplinary environmental science program.

The new department name provoked controversy. Three potato scientists suggested the name "Department of Horticulture, Landscape Architecture, and Potatoes" instead. Accreditation be damned, they argued, potato research brought in more funding than landscape architecture ever would. I was intrigued. Potato science did not exist as a discipline at Penn. I thought a depart-

mental letterhead including spuds would be rather funky, so I voted with the three potato scientists. Alas, we lost thirty to four, but I could always count on three votes for whatever I proposed over my next ten years in the Palouse.

My experiences with landscape architecture education at Washington State, and later at the University of Pennsylvania (1983-84) and the University of Colorado at Denver (1987-89), contributed to my recruitment in 1989 as chair of the Department of Planning at Arizona State University. My Arizona State colleagues also wanted to establish an accredited degree in landscape architecture. The department had two faculty members with landscape architecture degrees. It also offered a degree with a convoluted title: a B.S. in Design with an urban planning major and a landscape architecture concentration. One task was to convince the University of Arizona that we should be permitted to create a landscape architecture degree. Our provost had been told by his peers at the University of Arizona that we had greater likelihood to establish a medical degree at Arizona State. Fortunately, I had a positive relationship with senior University of Arizona faculty members Erv Zube and Bill Havens through the Council of Educators in Landscape Architecture. At the time, their faculty was considering dropping its bachelor's degree to focus on graduate offerings. They agreed not to oppose our B.S. in

CREATION OF A NEW DEGREE PROGRAM

Frederick R. Steiner

Landscape Architecture on the condition that we would not pursue a master's degree. We agreed, though my counterpart in architecture, Roger Schluntz, suggested that we had made a mistake and should have held out for an MLA.

In 1996, I served as an advisor to the University of New Mexico on their goal to establish an MLA. A former University of Pennsylvania student, Kim Sorvig, was on the faculty, and a former Arizona State colleague, Dick Eribes, was dean. In a series of academic musical chairs, Dick became dean at the University of Arizona, and Roger Schluntz took his place at the University of New Mexico. J. B. Jackson had passed away in August 1996, leaving the latter an endowment to help create an MLA. Its first chair was Alf Simon, on whose dissertation committee in geography I had served at Arizona State.

Back at Arizona State, we changed the name of the department to the School of Planning and Landscape Architecture (no potatoes this time). With the support of the dean of the College of Architecture and Environmental Design, John Meunier, we added faculty and successfully stood for accreditation.

At the University of Texas at Austin, the School of Architecture had a long-standing interest in establishing a landscape architecture degree program. Several landscape architects had served on the faculty, and several landscape archi-

tecture courses had been offered over the years. The interest came from at least two sources. First, green design had become a major scholarly pursuit in the School of Architecture. The faculty and alumni had helped pioneer Austin's green building program. The faculty believed that a landscape architecture program would enhance this green scholarly agenda. Second, the architecture and the planning programs had grown closer within the School. They believed that adding landscape architecture would strengthen this bridge between the architects and planners.

In the meanwhile, three landscape architecture degree programs already existed in Texas, and that number was viewed as an obstacle. Even so, interest in a new program contributed to my appointment in 2001 as dean of the School of Architecture at Austin. Soon after my arrival, a coalition of faculty organized the new Center for Sustainable Development, and the School renamed its M.S. in Architectural Studies-Design with Climate degree an M.S. in Sustainable Design.

To jumpstart landscape architecture, I decided to use our well-endowed Ruth Carter Stevenson Chair to attract Laurie Olin to campus. The offer I made to Laurie was to be our Richard Haag. Haag taught landscape architecture within architecture at the University of Washington. He had converted an amazing group of archi-tects—including Laurie Olin himself, as well as Bob

Hanna, Grant Jones, Ilze Jones, Jerry Diethelm, and Frank James, among others—to become landscape architects. He also taught scores of Northwest architects to appreciate landscape. As Laurie and I discussed the prospects, it became clear that he could not teach a complete studio, but he could be involved in a studio and deliver a series of lectures. Fortunately, a Hanna/Olin protégé, Gary Smith, happened to live in Austin. Gary had taught at the Universities of Pennsylvania and Delaware and had a distinguished small practice focused on botanical gardens. Gary agreed to teach a studio in cooperation with Laurie, who became our 2002 Ruth Carter Stevenson Chair and offered a series of stimulating lectures.

In preparing our proposal, I visited other landscape architecture programs around the state.

Texas Tech and A&M invited me to present lectures. At the latter, I had my photograph taken with Dean Tom Regan, who remarked "this will record when the Aggies gave the Longhorns a landscape architecture degree." With eight architecture programs in the state, four landscape architecture programs seemed reasonable. States with populations close in size to that of Texas (*e.g.*, California, New York) have similar numbers of landscape architecture programs, and Texans do not relish being second.

Ultimately, our proposal to establish an MLA sailed through the approval process, receiving unanimous support from both the architecture and the planning faculties, as well as from the School of Architecture as a whole. No one could recall another proposal receiving such overwhelming

approval from all the faculty members within the School. Likewise, the MLA proposal received strong support from university officials, including Graduate School Dean Theresa Sullivan and Provost Sheldon Ekland-Olson, who committed the resources to hire the faculty necessary to offer the degree. They saw how landscape architecture would contribute to the School's sustainability agenda. They also found compelling my argument that landscape architecture overlaps with both architecture and planning, and thus complements both. My colleague, Simon Atkinson, shepherded the proposal through all levels of the university, and it was endorsed by the University of Texas system, which in turn recommended it for state-level approval. All went well until December 2002. As it turned out, the University of Texas at Austin

had not proposed a new master's degree in some time. Procedures had changed, and a new state official was assigned our case. The process slowed down, and we produced new forms almost daily.

My fear was that the Texas legislature would be back in session in January, and our proposal for a new degree would be politicized. As a result, Sheldon Ekland-Olson, Simon Atkinson, and I pressed our case. Fortunately, the graduate school dean, Terry Sullivan, had been promoted as chief academic officer for the University of Texas system. The last item she approved at the campus had been our MLA proposal. The first case she was responsible for at the system level was our MLA proposal. With Terry's support, the degree was approved just before Christmas. My fears about the Texas legislature, which meets every other year, proved to be well founded. They made deep cuts in funding for the University of Texas. We had a new degree with scant resources. Thanks to our provost's support, we had a position which we filled with Hope Hasbrouck, who had a commitment to teach at the Harvard Graduate School of Design for another year and will join the Texas faculty in Fall 2004.

Our original proposal had been to offer both a first professional degree as well as a post-professional degree. Because of our constrained budget, I decided to offer only one of those tracks. We were swamped with applications both because of our location in Austin and because of the excellent reputation of our architecture and planning degrees. Given the strength of the first professional degree applications, I chose to focus on it for our first class. Nevertheless, Simon Atkinson pushed for accepting some post-professional candidates and, in the end, we accepted a class of first professional degree candidates and one post-professional candidate. The first class included individuals with a Ph.D., a J.D., an M.B.A., and an M.A. in botany. Others had strong experience in the fine arts and public relations. One is an E.R. nurse.

With Hope still in Cambridge, Simon Atkinson designed an innovative module system to offer studios and courses. We were able to draw on our architecture and planning faculty as well as talented Austin practitioners, such as Gary Smith and Jill Nokes. From Colorado, Design Workshop principals Kurt Culbertson and Todd Johnson contributed, as did Texas A&M professor Robin Abrams. Simon is an endowed professor and used his endowment to take our first class to London to initiate the year. By setting the stage in London, Simon underscored the relevance of landscape architecture as an urban design profession. Whereas most landscape architecture curricula begin in a greenfield, ours began at London Bridge Station. We further enhanced the design skills of the new class through the efforts and drawing acumen of architect Kimberly Kohlhas.

Unlike the landscape architecture programs at other leading public research universities, such as Illinois and Berkeley, ours is very new. Still, we have a strong foundation on which to build. Austin is well known for its environmentalism, our School

of Architecture for its design leadership, our community and regional planning program for its expertise in public participation, and the University of Texas for its leadership in the humanities and science. Our goal is to build on Austin institutions such as the Lady Bird Johnson Wildflower Center and the Charles Moore Center for the Study of Place, as well as the strengths of our architecture and planning programs and the University of Texas at Austin.

Importantly, our School of Architecture has no departments. One of my colleagues calls our structure "chauvinistically undepartmentalized." Thus, landscape architecture is a program in our School with several others: architecture, community and regional planning, architectural history, sustainable design, historic preservation, and interior design. The School-wide faculty created the landscape architecture program and remain active in its evolution. As we add landscape architects to our faculty, my hope is that they will contribute to these other programs and that faculty and students will advance their own disciplines while informing and being informed by the others in the School of Architecture.

Frederick R. Steiner, *Master of Community Planning (University of Cincinnati), Master of Regional Planning (University of Pennsylvania), M.A. and Ph.D. City and Regional Planning (University of Pennsylvania), is Dean of the School of Architecture at the University of Texas at Austin.*

DISCIPLINARY TRANSFORMATION AND THE DUAL M.ARCH./MLA PROGRAM AT PENN

Since the late 1990s, the departments of architecture and landscape architecture in the School
of Design at the University of Pennsylvania have
experienced a rapid increase of symbiotic, even
co-evolutionary collaboration, a process largely
shaped by student interest and commitment. The
two departments had collaborated in many prop-
erly collegial ways over the years, mounting joint
studios, encouraging cross-listed courses, making
joint faculty appointments, and even discussing the
formation of a common foundation studio (never
realized). Yet, despite the many initiatives, the
two departments retained their own quite distinct
studio and student cultures, oriented according
to the differences of their respective professional
communities.

A renewed commitment to inter-depart-
mental collaboration began to develop with the
appointment of Gary Hack as Dean, followed by
the selection of Richard Wesley as head of the
department of architecture, and then by James
Corner as chair of the department of landscape
architecture. Among their collective initiatives,
the most significant proved to be an arrangement developed between Wesley and Corner that
allowed students to attain a professional masters
degree in both departments in four years. Each
degree on its own normally requires three years
of study. However, over the years, a handful of
students had negotiated with the two departments
to count various courses towards both degrees
and so to reduce the total time of study. The final
breakthrough came when Richard Wesley crafted
a proposal according to which students would
complete the first two studios in both departments over two years, then undertake one studio
in each department during their third year, and two
more jointly counted studios in their fourth year.
Students still complete all the required course
work in both departments, but trade most of their
elective credits to do so.

Over the past four years, the number of students in the dual-degree program has grown
steadily, initially attracting students already in
one department to apply to the other, but quickly
becoming an attractive option for new students,
who apply to both departments simultaneously.
At present, there are twenty-six students in the
program (with five more offered admission for next
fall), which is just over ten percent of the students
in the masters of architecture program and over
twenty percent of those in landscape architecture.
While this condition is still quite new and its full
effects are just being realized, the back-and-forth
travel of these students between the two studio
cultures is certainly altering the boundary that has
existed between them. Their experiences do seem
to depend on their initial point of entry. As one
architecture student observed,

William W. Braham

"landscape opened my eyes to ideas of change and process that have started to challenge my approach towards architecture. Now in my architecture projects I am approaching design as a process that takes into consideration change of space, perception and materiality. The architecture department's focus on material exploration has allowed me to understand more directly this consideration of time and change both in architecture and the environment."

From the other point of entry, another student explained that

"landscape offers a material and ecological sensibility capable of expressing itself at many scales. [And] the architecture in this project benefits from the organizational strategies of landscape architecture, but materializes through the specific training in architecture that focuses on tectonics and technology. [T]he combination of training from the architecture department that considers tectonics, materiality, construction and technology with the training from the landscape architecture department that focuses on large scale organization and ecology fully compliment one another."

The work of the students in this combined program suggests a renewed commitment to the idea that similar design practices can operate on buildings, landscapes, and cities alike. However, unlike the older proposition that cities and spoons merely offered different scales of the same design problem, students traveling between architecture and landscape architecture apparently learn to shift codes, scales, and velocities in their thinking, acknowledging the disciplinary differences even as they transform them.

William W. Braham, *M. Arch., Ph.D. Arch., is Associate Chair of the Department of Architecture at the University of Pennsylvania School of Design.*

Kevin Fennell, third year of dual-degree program, final project from "Multiversity."

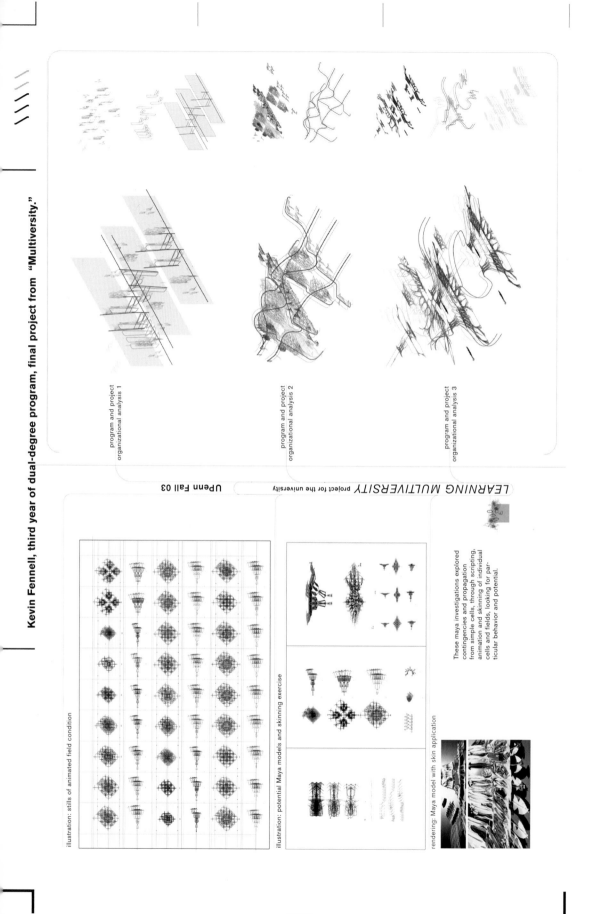

program and project
organizational analysis 1

program and project
organizational analysis 2

program and project
organizational analysis 3

UPenn Fall 03

project for the university *LEARNING MULTIVERSITY*

illustration: stills of animated field condition

illustration: potential Maya models and skinning exercise

These maya investigations explored contingencies and propagation from simple cells, through scripting, animation and skinning of individual cells and fields, looking for particular behavior and potential.

rendering: Maya model with skin application

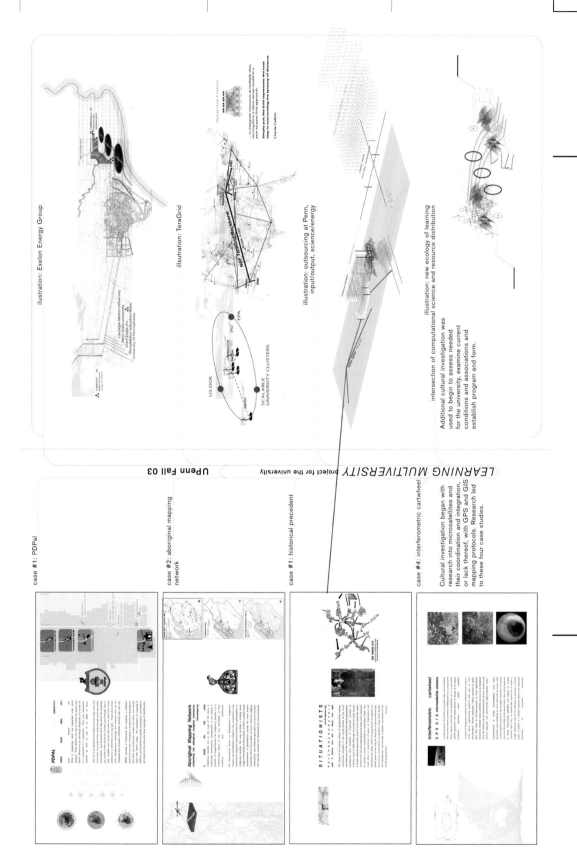

illustration: Exelon Energy Group

illsutration: TeraGrid

illustration: outsourcing at Penn,
input/output, science/energy

illustration: new ecology of learning
intersection of computational science and resource distribution

Additional cultural investigation was
used to begin to assess needed
for the university, examine current
conditions and associations and
establish program and form.

Cultural investigation began with
research into microsatellites and
their coordination and integration,
or lack thereof, with GPS and GIS
mapping protocols. Research led
to these four case studies.

LEARNING MULTIVERSITY

project for the university

UPenn Fall 03

case #1: PDPal

case #2: aboriginal mapping
network

case #1: historical precedent

case #4: interferometric cartwheel

PDPAL

Aboriginal Mapping Network

SITUATIONISTS

interferometric   cartwheel
G P S   G I S   microsatellite clusters

TEACHING LANDSCAPE WITHIN ARCHITECTURE: IN SEARCH OF THE COMMON GROUND

It is *all* design. That is the premise under which I have restructured a twenty-year-old minor curriculum in landscape architecture in the Department of Architecture and Interior Design at Miami University. I have been told numerous times that my situation at Miami is unique, and I have to admit I find that disheartening, an unfortunate "truth" that contributes to the persistence of the disparity between the design disciplines. My experience in practice taught me that landscape is too often seen as the "inferior" craft. Why should this be so? Without site context, architecture has no grounding, perhaps no real meaning? *Techne* without *Poiesis*. Why do not more architecture programs embrace the understanding of landscape and site *poiesis* alongside the necessary structure courses? Therefore, my goal with this minor has been not only to inform students about landscape *issues*, but also to minimize the boundaries and illustrate to students that it indeed is all design while at the same time fostering respect for the specialties of the individual design discipline.

My education had positioned architecture alongside landscape, having learned about significant architectural precedents as part of the landscape context. It taught me to see that the constructed landscape is a form of architecture, utilizing change as an integral building component. How then could I teach students to value and seek the integration of landscape with architecture? What it did not mean for me was a focus on landscape. Many times during those first classes students would tell me they were in my class primarily to "learn how to do a planting design." When I would tell these students that plants were ten percent of a landscape architect's job, their confusion was evident. It seemed to me that the focus for a revised minor curriculum needed to illustrate the overlap between landscape and architecture in such a way as to teach students more about design and, ultimately, to help them understand that true architecture is not a static object without context.

The Department of Architecture and Interior Design is an integrated program that strives to create interdisciplinary opportunities between the design disciplines. To that end, my involvement with the Department serves to extend that mission at both the undergraduate and graduate levels. In addition to the minor curriculum, a yearly landscape studio for undergraduates is offered and open to any architecture major. Non-architecture majors in the landscape minor may also have an opportunity to participate in the landscape studio with special permission. In addition, the three-year M.Arch. program intersects with the culminating core course of the minor curriculum, providing a unique opportunity for undergraduates to mix with grads and learn from their increased critical perspective. In Fall 2003, all students in the

Kimberly Hill

department were invited to participate in a landscape master plan design competition for a new world engine plant being constructed in Dundee, Michigan, by DaimlerChrysler Corporation. We had eight volunteers (all non-minors) and placed an impressive second in a pool of ten invited schools that included the top landscape programs in the region. These are just a few examples of how I seek to expand the interdisciplinary opportunities. Many more ventures have been explored and more are "on the table." As a result, the visibility and interest in the minor has increased not only within the Department of Architecture and Interior Design but across the campus, and I am increasingly finding myself talking with students who are interested in coming to Miami because of the landscape minor. I consider that quite an achievement.

Structure and Methodology

The primary model for the new curriculum of the landscape minor was my own educational experience at the Harvard Graduate School of Design, where I earned my Master of Landscape Architecture. The landscape program at the GSD was, at its core, a design theory education that illuminated the connections between the design disciplines. When I started teaching at Miami, it

was a surprise to discover that I often knew more about architecture than my architecture majors. Consequently, I thought this could prove to be an advantage in teaching students to value landscape as more than planting design. Therefore, I strove to create an integrated approach that would focus on the commonality of design and theory through critical architectural precedents.

At the heart of the revised curriculum is a solid core of new landscape courses, housed in the Architecture program, which build off one another to provide students with a foundation in progressive development of design theory. One course remains from the old core curriculum: an introduction to landscape and urban design, required at the sophomore level in the architecture curriculum and taught by another faculty member. There were no existing syllabi to work from for the two courses I had inherited. I therefore had the rare opportunity to build from the ground up. From these two core courses, which provided a technical and historical balance, I sought to build a compliment of courses that would focus on increasing landscape awareness and understanding, knowledge of basic construction methods and materials, planting theories, history, and design theory. The curriculum is rounded out with three interdepartmental and interdivisional courses in two support categories, one in plant science (housed in Botany), and the other in a focus category which allows the student to choose courses according to their interests in one of several supporting disciplines such as botany, geology, urban studies, or anthropology.

Pedagogy

The sequencing of the core is intended not only to increase the professional content of the curriculum but also to expand the students' awareness of the potential avenues of interest in landscape architecture, since the profession is so broad in scope. There is no studio requirement in the minor because non-architecture majors would not typically be able to enroll. Therefore, to introduce design process, most of the core courses include studio-like design problems of varying types and depth. This way, architecture majors develop a stronger understanding of the link between their classes and their studios, while non-architecture majors get a sense of what design activity involves. At Harvard, I had the experience of finding myself in my first ever studio setting at a loss as to how I was to approach this new educational experience. Since many of the students enrolling in the minor are curious about the possibility of further education in landscape, my intent is to provide them with a mini-design program experience in an effort to prepare them better for a master's program in design.

The core sequence begins with the strengthening of awareness. Students get their first introduction to the issues and principles of landscape and urban design in ARC211, which provides an investigation into the architecture of the larger environment. Students are exposed to important precedents, case studies, and design environment problems in their own backyard by working in teams to think critically about spatial issues. The courses at the junior level (ARC335/336) build awareness with further inquiries into the psychological and technical issues of landscape experience. Explorations of cultural and physical landscape concerns are conducted through field walks, theoretical and poetic writings, and technical and design exercises.

In ARC335, *Landscape: Inquiry and Experience*, I draw on student's personal experiences through journaling, writing, and the arts as vehicles or lenses through which to expose and explore environmental and cultural values. A critical key in this class is to build from the myriad of experiences students already possess in relation to landscape space as a means to increase awareness of the diversity of issues one must consider when designing public space, landscape, and architecture. Students must become aware that their own way of seeing things is like viewing the world with blinders on. My goal is for students to recognize their preconceptions and limitations *because* of their experiences, while at the same time, providing validation of those experiences. Through the constant sharing of individual viewpoints in class discussion and exchanged writing assignments, students become aware that even within a fairly cohesive cultural context—upper-middle class, mid-western, white, suburban—there is a high degree of diversity in landscape experience and desire for designed and natural space. As a result of this class, most students, if not all have a deeper understanding of themselves and their values in relation to the issues of design, landscape, architecture, and the cultural context within which they find themselves. Quite often, students come to this class simply testing-the-waters of their interest in landscape, and this may be the only chance I have to make an impact on how a young person sees, and ultimately impacts their world. Therefore, I hope to deconstruct a student's perception of their known world and help them to realize that there are always more questions, more viewpoints, than solutions.

The one technical course in the curriculum (ARC336) explores the construction and manipulation of landscape form through grading, materials, and architectural constructions. Students often learn a great deal of respect for the landscape profession through this course because they find the process of grading so challenging. I also find the class challenging to teach, preferring the theoretical realm of design to the technical. Therefore, I use the course to develop the connection between the abstract realm of perception and technical reality through several design exercises that serve to increase students' awareness of the ways in which built reality influences the psychological impact of landscape space. Key assignments towards this goal begin with a photo essay assignment intended to increase awareness of landscape construction. A compare/contrast exercise follows in which students choose a detail of landscape construction (*e.g.*, steps, curbs, seating) and formulate critical judgments of success and failure between two existing conditions through technical drawings, photographs, and sketches, along with written descriptions of their experience of the two spaces. Lastly, students choose a construction material—concrete, metal, brick, or wood—and complete an analytical photo essay on the impacts of that material in designed landscape space. My goal in this course is for students to become not technically proficient but more *aware*, and therefore more sensitive to the built landscape environment.

Plants in Design (ARC430) is structured as a half-semester sprint course, meeting two hours, once a week for seven weeks. This is an intense, studio-like setting that investigates the basic ideological, conceptual, and technical issues that affect and influence planting designs—my answer to the "how do I do a planting design?" question. When I was in practice, I began planting designs with a conception of how "architectural" space is shaped via scale, texture and color. The appropriate plants are then found to create this conceived space. I illustrate this process by taking students through four design exercises where they develop sketch models to explore plant architectural space. Students are first introduced to historical plant typologies and then choose two typologies for combination, such as alleé and grove, and explore the possibilities for discovering architectural space through variations in scale, texture, and color. The class runs informally, sitting on the floor surrounding the gathered models as we discuss each model as a class, sharing readings and intentions. This format serves to expand the possibilities and potential for exploration and students report the discussion sessions are the most valuable learning experience in the class.

The culminating class in the core curriculum, entitled *Theory and History of Landscape Architecture* (ARC435/535), is a split class of undergraduate and first-year graduate students. Although we focus on the historical development and transitions of the major eras in garden design, strong ties are made with architecture and the overlap between the practice of architecture and landscape. I am not a historian, and there is much I would need to learn to give history its due intellectual justice. However, I do enjoy pondering design history in the way pieces of art, religion, politics, and literature fit together like a puzzle. Therefore, this class models the puzzle as a means of teaching the process of theory in design. I serve to enlighten students as to the value of theory, showing them how theoretical process plays out in history, and illustrating why theory is not optional in design process. For the last four years, I have continued to subtract historical material in favor of class discussion and the illustration of theory as a social process. My ultimate goal is not for students to memorize the details of history, but to understand the necessity of asking questions in design process and the appropriate use of historical precedent.

Many design practitioners today tend to reject theory, and many students tend to think of it as a four-letter-word. In my opinion, those attitudes, combined with lack of awareness about how the design disciplines fit together, foretell a grim future for design. Therefore, as I have continued to develop and refine the landscape minor curriculum, it has become apparent to me that the value of that curriculum is not exclusively in educating students about landscape, but about design in general, what it means, and how it ties with social context and everyday life. To teach students to become more critical of the marks they will make on the world is a gift to us all. To teach design students to become more aware of the overlaps between the design disciplines will greatly serve to strengthen the professions.

Kimberly Hill, *MLA (Harvard), is an Assistant Professor and the Coordinator of Landscape Studies in the Department of Architecture and Interior Design at Miami University.*

Aerial view of the one-mile by one-mile
sectional grid that organizes much of the
American landscape.
photo: Jeffrey L. Day

TWO FACTS CONCERNING LANDSCAPE IN ARCHITECTURE

Jeffrey Day

"The certainty of the absolute garden will never be regained." [1]

///// Robert Smithson

A collaboration between Min|Day, an architectural practice, and *FACT*, a student-staffed design-construct lab at the University of Nebraska, *Bemis = Art Landscape* is the first phase of a master plan and projects for the Bemis Center for Contemporary Arts in Omaha, Nebraska. To address an indeterminate project with a long-term schedule for completion, the design team employed strategies and concepts more familiar in landscape planning, where uncertainty is common.

The project is currently beginning its first construction phase and work is progressing on the design of future phases. This essay describes the concepts and principles that underlie the master plan and their origin in late-twentieth-century notions of landscape. It concludes with a look at a follow-up project, a proposal for Art Farm, in which we apply similar tactics over a much broader field. We maintain that a transgression of disciplinary tactics—landscape into architecture—offers a useful approach to complex projects. Furthermore, the collaboration between the academy and the profession, with the author as link, is crucial to the success of the projects.

" ...an endless feedback loop:
Past functioning has produced today's structure;
Today's structure produces today's functioning;
Today's functioning will produce future structure. " [2]

///// Richard T.T. Forman

Transgressing Practices

Architectural educators have long sought to fortify disciplinary boundaries
in an attempt to create their own mandate within the broader university
context. The emphasis on "professionalism" and "minimum competency"
found in many schools derives, in part, from outside pressures brought
to bear by the profession itself (*e.g.*, to satisfy the need for well-trained
employees). However, an increasing number of architectural commissions
and competitions demand cross-disciplinary thinking and the collaboration of various creative enterprises. The expert discourses of isolated
disciplines are no longer capable of acting alone in such a realm. Through
a series of collaborative projects that I have initiated at the University of
Nebraska College of Architecture, we are beginning to explore the possibilities for such disciplinary transgression.

I established *FACT*[3] in 2001 as an academic framework in which
to engage students in actual projects that demand the sort of tactical
thinking and collaboration that large-scale projects demand. In our situation, crossing disciplinary boundaries is even more of a challenge because
there is no Department of Landscape Architecture at our university upon
which we can depend for certain professional skills. We must be opportu-
nistic in our borrowing of techniques and processes from other disciplines,
such as landscape architecture, in order to be effective in our work on
projects that do not fit neatly into the bounds of conventional, segregated
practice. For these large-scale, long-lived projects, we seek an approach

to "master planning" that is flexible, open, and highly attuned to contingency. The work demands a mode of practice that resists the normative teleology of the architectural profession's preferred means, and landscape architecture seems to offer some potential.

In the projects undertaken by *FACT*, landscape is understood not through its origin in the visual (in landscape painting and scenery), but in its procedural function. As Stan Allen has written recently, "landscape is not only a formal model for urbanism today, but perhaps more importantly, a model for process."[4] This view gained popularity in the 1990s not only in academia but also in practice, where large, phased projects demanded an approach more forgiving than the normative procedures of architecture would allow. Landscape architecture, or more specifically the sub-disciplines of land planning and landscape ecology, appeared to offer the greatest potential. *FACT* seizes on procedures and representational tactics that deny the fixed point of view and the static frame: suggestive diagrams as opposed to fixed perspective views, models on which nothing is glued down, and discontinuous montages formed of loosely composed images. These and other procedures are at once tools for presenting design proposals and tricks to keep the designers from becoming enchanted by their own illusions.

While these hybrid representational tactics are now common to many design fields, the organizational strategies that we employ are clearly based in landscape. More specifically, our projects trace their lineage to the vernacular landscapes of the Great Plains, to the history of adaptation and inhabitation of the gridded surfaces that dominate this vast part of the American Midwest. For insights into this landscape, we look back to the writings of J.B. Jackson:

" …landscape is not scenery, it is not a political unit; it is really no more than a collection, a system of man-made spaces on the surface of the earth. Whatever its shape or size it is never simply a natural space, a feature of the environment; it is always artificial, always synthetic, always subject to sudden or unpredictable change. " [5]

///// J.B. Jackson

Vernacular Landscapes

The word landscape, while open to multiple definitions, debates, and interpretations, can best be summed up by J.B. Jackson's proposed formula, *"landscape as a composition of man-made spaces on the land."*[6] The important feature of Jackson's concept of landscape is its emphasis on the artificial and synthetic quality of space. Landscape is not a variant of the concept of nature as something external to human agency, but rather an organized system of spaces imposed upon a "natural" environment. Furthermore, a vernacular landscape is defined more by relationships between individuals and their changing needs than

by political will. Landscape is the physical manifestation of the human attempt to control time; as Jackson points out, "a landscape is thus a space deliberately created to speed up or slow down the process of nature."[7] By extension, Jackson's theory of the synthetic, process-based vernacular landscape subjects towns and cities to the same descriptive as the vegetal surfaces of the rural environment. While not the activist, critical apparatus of a contemporary landscape urbanist,[8] Jackson's observational theory is valuable for its explanations of the expedient underpinnings of the everyday environment and the improvisational tactics it betrays.

In his attempt to historicize the vernacular landscape as a *concept* (in contrast to the *phenomena* of landscapes), Jackson suggests that three phases or distinct concepts of landscape emerged over the course of western history. The medieval landscape, which he calls Landscape One, was characterized by mobility, a mixing of uses, and a lack of clearly articulated symbolic meaning.[9] Landscape Two, first appearing in the Renaissance,[10] privileged the ideal view and gave rise to the definition of landscape as scenery. Jackson writes, "Unlike Landscape One, which mixed all kinds of uses and spaces together, Landscape Two insists on spaces which are homogenous and devoted to a single purpose."[11] Le Notre's Vaux-le-Vicomte and other European classicizing monuments fit this tradition with their emphasis on the legibility of an ordered environment and on clearly defined symbolic hierarchies. Jackson finds the apotheosis of Landscape Two—and the greatest manifestation of a classical political landscape—in the grid system imposed over much of the United States by Thomas Jefferson's 1785 National Land Survey.

That decentralized grid still provides the basic, large-scaled order found in the Great Plains. However, the same grid system is part of the downfall of Landscape Two and the notion of the "sanctity of place."[12] Although the grid was expected to discourage large-scale land speculation and thereby create a democratic (and not aristocratic) landscape based on the simple ordered form of the square, it promoted a far more mobile and mutable community with much weaker ties to place. Easily divisible and transferable property, the railroads and advancements in communication, and new methods of construction (*e.g.*, the balloon frame) led to a dissolution of the stable landscape of Jefferson's vision. These are some of the factors that Jackson cites as leading to Landscape Three, a new paradigm that is developing along lines more similar to the medieval landscape (Landscape One) than to Landscape Two.[13] This paradigm, arguably the dominant force in land development and the perception of landscape, capitalizes on the flexible, and disinter-

ested, generic form of the grid. The grid is now the regulating line for unlimited potential. Certainly the sprawling cities of the central and southern Great Plains (including Chicago) attest to this.

Our interest in this discourse is more than purely historical. Whereas Jefferson's delineation of the grid was a finite cognitive act, the operative fact of the grid continues to dominate the process of inhabitation in the majority of the continental United States. In regions devoid of extreme topography (the Great Plains, for example), position supersedes place as the locus of inhabitation. The lines of the grid are the infrastructure of settlement.

FACT$_1$: Bemis = Art Landscape

Established in Omaha the early 1980s, the Bemis Center for Contemporary Arts is one of the premier artist residency programs in the United States. While the Bemis's primary mission is to provide time and space for artistic practice to flourish, the Center supplements that role with a commitment to supporting public educational programs and a series of innovative contemporary art exhibitions. In 2001, the Bemis approached Min|Day and *FACT* with the desire to initiate an expansion of its current facility with the understanding that the work would occur over an extended period of time. The range of individual projects would involve landscape design, new construction, interior architecture, graphics, and in-depth event programming. The challenge was to accommodate multiple needs, diverse personalities, and flexible processes within a single project.

Our approach was to imagine the Bemis not as a static container for art, but as a dynamic, transmutable landscape within which art occurs. Following J.B. Jackson, we proceed from an understanding of landscape as an artificial and mutable productive field. Like Jackson's, ours is a landscape of cultivation. Unlike conventional understandings of architecture as a fixed, ordered whole, landscape is seen as an organizational system designed to accommodate change. This conception of landscape does not distinguish between natural topographies and built structures, nor does it allow organic or inorganic materials to occupy privileged positions within the milieu of the *art landscape*. Concepts adapted from landscape ecology (*e.g.*, patches, corridors, boundaries, and mosaics)[14] and from mereotopology[15] provide a theoretical framework for a design process that uses landscape as a model for architecture and building programming. That model, inspired by the Jeffersonian grid of the Great Plains landscape, allowed us to create an adaptable infrastructure for a project that will be actualized over time and is subject to constant forces of change

site plan

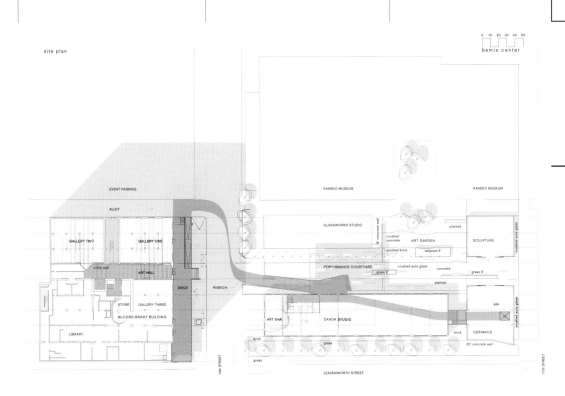

and indeterminacy. The project begins with an analysis of existing uses, functions, desires, and material assets and proceeds to construct a new organizational framework that can accommodate both these known conditions and the ultimately unknowable possible futures of the Bemis Center.

In contrast to modernist notions of neutral space and the centrality of the art object, we propose the "art landscape" as a non-centered field in which diverse art practices can flourish. Contemporary art practice increasingly repudiates "objecthood" and fixed points of reference in favor of art that is open to multiple meanings and het- erogeneous experiences. We attempt to accom- modate this difficult situation by proposing spaces that are forever transformed by the practices taking place within them.

Following Jefferson's generic landscape system, and the operative regulating line of Le Corbusier (for whom the "regulating line is a guar- antee against willfulness"[16]), we adopted the stra- tegic understanding that this project will very likely continue to develop after we are gone. Our desire to have lasting influence must take the form of a strong but supple organizational system that will both accommodate change and structure its mani- festation. Our greatest task is to provide limits on the willful formalism of subsequent developments. The notion of the art landscape encompasses not only the mutable field of the projected Art Garden

but also the interior space of the existing McCord- Brady and Okada Buildings. A hierarchical infra- structure of regulating lines (distinguished by both crisp and indeterminate boundaries) derived from existing structures encompasses the mosaic of surface patches that organize and contain spaces for art making, art display, and residence. These diverse spaces for art (which we call the Art Fog) are tied together by the Art Hall and by the Orange Ribbon. An extension of the existing cen- tral hall of the McCord-Brady Building, the Art Hall is a continuous corridor-like space that extends from a pavilion on the roof of the McCord-Brady Building to a kiln in a proposed new building to the east of the Okada. Around this spine or Ribbon, we have organized all of the existing and new spaces and programs of the Bemis Center for Contemporary Art.

We envision the Bemis as an invigorating environment created out of the energies of artists and the raw materials they find around them- selves, be they physical or virtual. Expanding on the history of many Bemis artists recycling found materials, we propose using a vast array of mate- rials reclaimed from demolition sites (*e.g.*, crushed brick, auto glass) along with products created out of recycled waste (*e.g.*, plastic wood, strawboard, high fly-ash concrete). The arrangement of these materials in the field is limited by the bounds of the surface alone, not by an *a priori* composi-

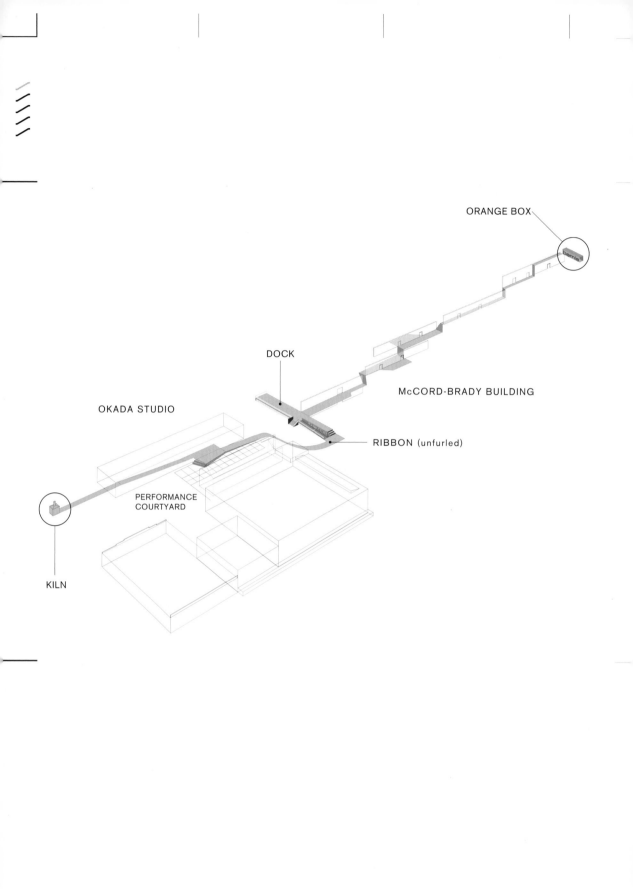

ORANGE BOX

DOCK

McCORD-BRADY BUILDING

OKADA STUDIO

RIBBON (unfurled)

PERFORMANCE
COURTYARD

KILN

tional order laid down by the architectural team. Additionally, the Art Garden will be planted with species native to the Great Plains, yet organized in a pattern more familiar in modern agricultural cultivation. The McCord-Brady roof will have a planted surface to control run-off and provide grounds for cultivating produce. Wind generators will serve the power needs of the Bemis while providing a visible demonstration of a new paradigm for urban energy production.

As a framework for the long-term expansion goals of the Bemis Center, *Bemis = Art Landscape* is a non-teleological master plan, one with discrete points of reference but no finite end. It is a collection of independent projects within a field that, like the gridded Great Plains, is constantly changing yet always retains a certain organizational rigor. Specific projects such as the new entrance/loading dock for the McCord-Brady Building, the ramp/performance space for the Okada Building, the Art Garden, the new Ceramics/Sculpture Studio, the Art Hall with its undulating Utility Wall, and the third, fourth, and fifth floor interiors will be realized over time, though not necessarily in any predictable order. Despite the inherent uncertainties of such an approach, the art landscape will always be the ultimate operative condition of the Bemis Center.

FACT$_2$: Art Farm

While the work at the Bemis Center is ongoing, *FACT* and Min|Day have begun a second long-term project with another Nebraska art institution. Art Farm is a non-profit art residency program situated on a forty-acre working farm in Marquette, Nebraska. In operation for just over ten years, Art Farm is very similar to the Bemis Center in its basic mission, though the physical character and context of its facilities are noticeably different. The site currently includes a large, informal sculpture "field" and approximately twenty separate standing and salvaged buildings. Our initial task is to create an organizational infrastructure that can both accommodate and structure the development of Art Farm over the next ten years. While we may be fortunate to design and construct several of the new buildings and modifications to those that exist, the very nature of Art Farm suggests that much of the work that follows will be the product of the improvisations of multiple participants.

After an initial survey of the landscape and existing buildings, and a detailed programmatic study, we began by proposing to drape an organizational net over the site. Derived from the local section lines, this grid creates a miniaturized facsimile of the Jeffersonian landscape that surrounds Art Farm. Rather than propose a generic grid of arbitrary dimension, we derived our grid

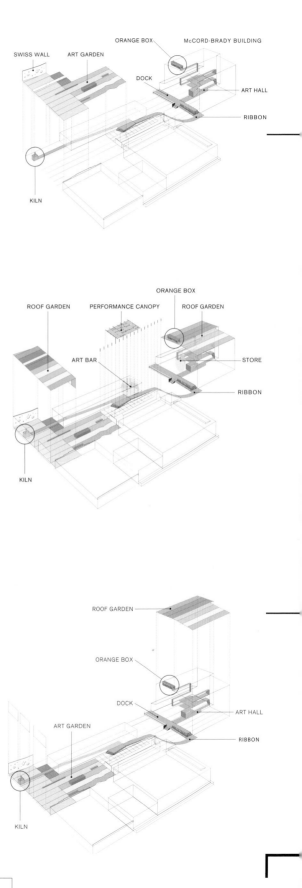

from the actual surrounding one-mile square sections, which we rescaled by a factor originating in the pole and the furlong,[17] the dimensions used to layout acreage. What became apparent in this process was the high degree of specificity that the supposedly generic grid actually possesses. Owing to the imprecision of nineteenth-century surveying techniques, the local section lines are not at all square. When one notes these circumstances, and the origin of the common units of measure employed in the landscape, one recognizes the very physical and non-arbitrary facts buried deep within what have become generic standards. (Of course, the metric system relishes its universality and arbitrariness). In a sense, Jefferson derived his utopian restructuring of the American landscape not from pure Platonic or Cartesian geometries per se but from the very tangible and earthly habits of farmers and the stamina of their oxen. As with all systems of order, the form outlives its practical origin.[18] At Art Farm, we wish to give these units new meaning by accentuating their innate specificity.

When these lines are first staked out on the actual site, they will not in any way be physicalized. Like the original National Land Survey, the lines are only a virtual infrastructure of fiat boundaries, awaiting inhabitation. Over time, our new grid of mini-sections will accumulate physical structures (built or planted form), slowly becoming more bona fide as they gradually manifest themselves in the landscape. The future of Art Farm will be a re-enactment of the settlement of the Great Plains.

" To propose a topography is to reject a topology. It is to consider that an understanding of contemporary architecture is not a question of logos, of universal ideas, but of graphe, of writings, of conventional and logical artifices by means of which a knowledge of the particular objects, of the architectures and the architects of the present moment may hope to become more veridical. " [19]

///// Ignasi de Solà-Morales Rubio

Concluding with Buildings...

Solà-Morales describes a crisis that surfaced in architectural theory in the 1950s (notably articulated by Nicholas Pevsner through his renewed interest in the picturesque tradition), during which many critics tried to reconcile a seeming inconsistency between modern buildings and their surroundings.[20] The attempt to create a picturesque continuum in which architectural artifacts lose their qualities as objects is evident in much of the building activity of the period, such as the

Case Study Houses and much of Frank Lloyd Wright's work. Perhaps this was, in part, a reaction against the classicism and rationalism of J.B. Jackson's Landscape Two. In comparison, Solà-Morales writes of the present condition, "today's landscape hardly constitutes a background into which the architectural object might be thought of as inserting, or integrating, or diffusing itself."[21] Seldom do contemporary buildings disappear into their surroundings, and the agricultural vernacular of the Great Plains is no exception. But it is exactly this discontinuity that forms what we call *landscape*. Landscape is no more a continuum of undifferentiated topographical flows than it is an ideal or inalienable natural backdrop for architecture (read "buildings"). Landscape is a constantly mutating force that yields little to rigid structures and almost always results in heterogeneity. This striated condition, I believe, renders the debate between the object building and the integrated building irrelevant. For this reason, we look to *landscape* practice for tools to help us make architecture more responsive to the durational aspects of inhabitation.

In the production of architecture, our only course is to operate on present topographical conditions in order to generate the possibility for new conditions. We have no recourse to universal truths or topologies, nor can our work as architects form a coherent part of a holistic vision of landscape. By custom and in practice, our activity is limited to the construction of palimpsests written over the particular spaces in the landscape where we choose (or are required) to act.

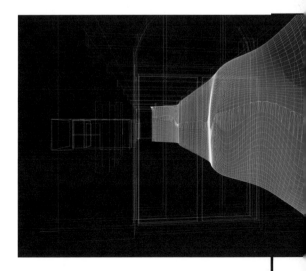

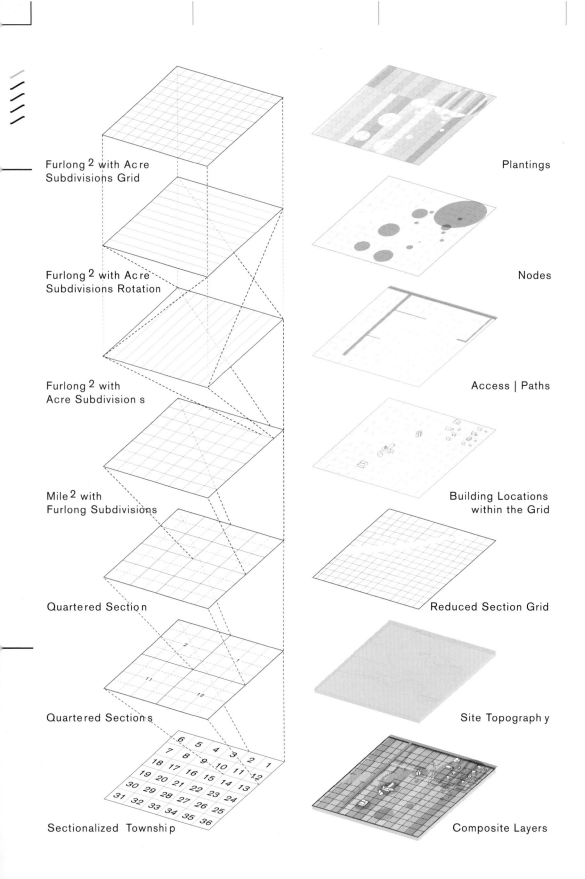

Furlong 2 with Acre
Subdivisions Grid

Plantings

Furlong 2 with Acre
Subdivisions Rotation

Nodes

Furlong 2 with
Acre Subdivisions

Access | Paths

Mile 2 with
Furlong Subdivisions

Building Locations
within the Grid

Quartered Section

Reduced Section Grid

Quartered Sections

Site Topography

Sectionalized Township

Composite Layers

Jeffrey L. Day, *M.Arch., is an Assistant Professor in the College of Architecture at the University of Nebraska-Lincoln. He is also a principle of Min|Day, a firm based in Omaha, Nebraska, and San Francisco, California.*

NOTES

1 _ Robert Smithson, "A Sedimentation of the Mind: Earth Projects," in Robert Smithson, *The Collected Writings*, ed. Jack Flam (Berkeley: University of California Press, 1996), 113.

2 _ Richard T.T. Forman and Michael Godron, *Landscape Ecology* (New York: John Wiley, 1986), 3.

3 _ *FACT* is the University of Nebraska College of Architecture's Fabrication And Construction Team. It is a design lab that offers students a forum for exploration aimed at expanding the understanding of the complex relationships between thinking (conceiving, designing, theorizing) and making. *FACT* engages design intensive projects and creative clients in collaborations that bridge the gap between design and construction. In such a practice, the boundaries that conventionally distinguish the profession of architecture are eroded to admit other disciplines ordinarily thought of as distinct (landscape, construction, and so on). In summary, *FACT* hopes to offer students the opportunity to explore a more fluid practice that integrates design and production. Such a practice allows production to influence design as much as design directs production, but in the end our goal is to educate designers, not builders. *FACT* frequently collaborates with the San Francisco-Omaha based architectural practice Min|Day.

4 _ Stan Allen, "Matt Urbanism: The thick 2-D," in *CASE: Le Corbusier's Venice Hospital*, ed Hashim Sarkis (Munich: Prestel, 2001), 125.

5 _ John Brinkerhoff Jackson, "Concluding with Landscapes," *Discovering the Vernacular Landscape* (New Haven: Yale University Press, 1984), 156.

6 _ Jackson,"The Word Itself," in *op. cit.*, 7.

7 _ Ibid., 8.

8 _ Cf. especially the writings and works of Charles Waldheim and James Corner.

9 _ Jackson, "Concluding with Landscapes," *op. cit.*, 152.

10 _ The manifestation of this idea seems to be most pronounced in Enlightenment or neoclassical concepts of landscape.

11 _ Jackson, "Concluding," 152.

12 _ Ibid.

13 _ Ibid., 154.

14 _ Richard T.T. Forman and M. Gordon, *Landscape Ecology* (New York: John Wiley, 1986).

15 _ A sub-field of formal ontology, mereotoplology provides the formal bases for describing parts and boundaries. The field is an alternative to set theory and is an elision of mereology (the theory of parts and wholes) and topology (the theory of boundaries and connection). See Barry Smith, "Mereotopology: A Theory of Parts and Boundaries," *Data and Knowledge Engineering* 20 (1996): 287-303.

16 _ Le Corbusier, *Towards a New Architecture*, trans. Frederick Etchells (New York: Dover Publications, 1931), 66.

17 _ A furlong, from "furrow long," is 660 feet, the length of furrow that oxen plow before they are rested and turned. An acre is a measure of area one furlong by 4 poles (rods, or 16.5 feet).

18 _ For example, the Los Angeles street grid is based on a convenient interval for trolley stops.

19. Ignasi de Solà-Morales Rubio, "Introduction," *Differences: Topographies of Contemporary Architecture* (Cambridge: MIT Press 1997), 6.

20 _ Ibid., 20.

21 _ Ibid., 21

COMMUNITY DESIGN

AS A VENUE FOR EXPLORING

INTERSTITIAL SPACE IN

ARCHITECTURAL AND LANDSCAPE

ARCHITECTURAL EDUCATION

Wendy McClure

Why Operate in the Community Context?

The community context can provide an effective forum in which to stage interdisciplinary collaborations and learning experiences between landscape architecture and architecture. At the University of Idaho, faculty and students in architecture and landscape have partnered with one another and with dozens of Northwest communities since 1987 to address key design and planning issues. Projects have included downtown revitalization, design of community gateways, civic centers, parks, office parks, interpretive centers, waterfront re-development, new town centers and improvements to highway strips.

The forum of community design creates win-win situations for interdisciplinary learning experiences. First, the process of service learning itself endows projects with a purpose above and beyond self-actualization. Second, community partners value the creative energy and insight students can offer, enabling students to make connections between design and public good. Third, the reality-charged context in which students must work is highly motivating, often inspiring a greater willingness to cross boundaries in order to formulate successful responses to community needs.

How Does the Community Design Process Work?

Community partners from throughout the inter-mountain West, including city planning offices, city councils, chambers of commerce and tribal governments, regularly contact our programs in architecture and landscape architecture for design and planning assistance. Participating faculty screen projects for their potential to meet the pedagogical goals of a studio as well as community expectations, and to ensure that adequate support is available to offset expenses. At the onset of each eight- to ten-week project, architecture and landscape architecture studios are merged and organized into interdisciplinary design teams of four to five students. During the first few weeks, each team researches key project-related issues and case studies in preparation for site visits. Their research informs design and becomes a resource for community partners. Students and faculty travel to the community settings for formal public and informal meetings with project stakeholders, site tours with community guides, and to document site conditions. Student presence in communities, as they document site conditions in a swat team like approach, generally attracts attention and enthusiastic response from community members. Once the teams return to campus, landscape architecture students lead architecture students through systematic and thorough site inventory and analysis processes. Together they establish project goals and develop initial site and programmatic responses. At the conclusion of four or five weeks, each team develops a master plan identifying key goals, overarching concepts for improvements and design interventions, and areas for focus development.

Faculty coordinators encourage pairs of students within each team to select one or more focus areas requiring collaborative, interdisciplinary design. Typical examples include a new civic center, a threshold to the community, an interpretive park system, a waterfront or resort development, the revitalization of main street, and improvements to an ailing historic downtown or highway strip. Students spend four to five weeks concentrating on these focus areas and preparing for public presentation to the community. The most successful presentations have been community-wide events featuring an open house potluck and evening presentations by each team. Final products include digital media presentations, project summary books, and/or websites.

Why is Community Design an Important Pedagogical Tool?

Community design projects foster mutual discoveries between architects and landscape architects. Teams that learn to draw on the strengths and expertise of both disciplines usually achieve the strongest results. The scale and scope of community projects falls literally and metaphorically in the space between design traditions of architecture and landscape architecture. Students and faculty must operate outside of traditional domains and explore an expanded palette of spatial components and design elements in order to address key programmatic issues adequately.

The process of community making requires injecting new vitality into the public realm, a neglected theater of community life. The focus is not on the building as an object to be "landscaped" but on establishing a positive dialogue among built elements. Students are encouraged to draw from the theoretical models and spatial language of interdisciplinary thinkers such as Kevin Lynch, Christopher Alexander, William Whyte, and Spiro Kostof to address the issues posed by repair of a degraded public realm. Definition of a positive public realm must engage the expertise of architects and landscape architects alike. Each spatial component, whether building, park, street, signage, plant material, or street furniture is valued for its contribution to community identity and aesthetics. Architecture students see how plant materials and ground planes can be manipulated to sculpt a complex and layered spatial environment. Landscape architecture students discover the role of building envelopes as mediators between exterior and interior space, not simply as boundaries, division points, or backdrops. Through collaboration, students realize the value of buildings as critical participants in designs for streetscapes, pocket parks, or plazas. They also learn that effective building design in the public realm should represent a complex negotiation between the demands of interior space and function and the external forces of site, context, and climate.

Studio education at the University of Idaho is built on a common foundation in fine arts in freshman year and divergence in sophomore year. Collaboration offers exposure of all students to discipline-specific approaches to creative problem-solving and meeting technological challenges. Ideally, students learn through teaching. Upper-level studio education in landscape architecture, for example, encourages a more reverent approach to site inventory and analysis as a precedent to preliminary design. Both programs emphasize sustainable approaches to design, providing students with opportunities to design around common values. In the community context, students are challenged to expand their understanding of sustainability beyond discipline-specific green building design or the maintenance of healthy ecological systems. Design and planning decisions must also support the preservation of regional identity, and promote economic and social well-being. Solutions must be inclusive, integrated, and solve multiple problems in the built environment.

Wendy McClure is a Professor in the Department of Architecture at the University of Idaho.

Figure 1. Student community design master plan.

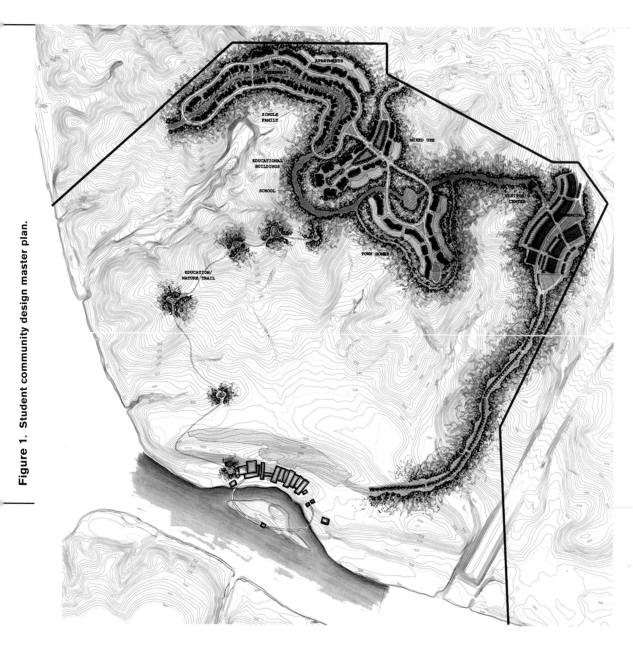

ENVIRONMENT + BUILT FORM: THE YORK COUNTY COLLABORATIVE STUDIO

José Cabán, Robert Hewitt, and Daniel Nadenicek

The phrase "Landscape within Architecture" suggests images of built form encompassing parcels of green space. Of course, landscape comprises living and dynamic systems that should influence the placement and interrelationships of the various architectural elements placed within it. This understanding was recently explored in a collaborative studio at Clemson University. In May of 2003, the Culture and Heritage Commission of York County, South Carolina, asked the School of Architecture and the Department of Planning and Landscape Architecture at Clemson to work on a community design for a 400-acre parcel along the Catawba River just north of Rock Hill, South Carolina. **[Fig. 1]** In Fall 2003, Clemson students in three concurrent studios engaged in a collaborative project inspired by an environmentally sensitive perspective on landscape and architecture. For that endeavor, Clemson also collaborated with architecture students and faculty from the University of North Carolina Charlotte.

Our involvement followed the design for a green museum and surrounding landscape produced several months earlier by William McDonough, a leading designer of green architecture, and Warren Byrd, a nationally recognized landscape architect and professor at the University of Virginia. Their work involved approximately forty acres of the site and was focused on natural expression and sustainability. **[Fig. 2]** The Culture

and Heritage Commission wanted the community design to be driven by the same focus on nature, with an emphasis on the earth's resources. This essay describes the studio-based project more fully and discusses the implications of the experience for the developing curricula within the School of Architecture and the Department of Planning and Landscape Architecture at Clemson.

The Architectural Response to Site and Landscape

In traditional urban architecture, buildings respond to site limitations as well as to local ordinances and codes. Contextual response is often limited to conditions of setting (*e.g.*, infill projects that are reduced to a façade expression) or lost to the iconic tendencies of modern commercial construction: the logo architecture of golden arches and other forms of overwhelming signage. Such buildings are endowed with a narrative that uses a commonly accepted vocabulary, and society has long established the terms for communication between the individual and this sort of built environment. While there is a value to society in the role of this architecture as a common ground accepted by most and understood by all, its practice produces a monotonous rhetoric and a set of practical rules that work against a true interaction

between site, program, and the intentions of the designer.

Response to urban context varies as dramatically as the range of settings considered urban. At one end of the spectrum, a high-density urban wall leads to two-dimensional manipulation of form and image creation driven by stylistic preferences, dramatic expressions of materiality, and iconic design. Context is defined solely in terms of surrounding massing and the markings and perforations of the adjacent building envelopes. Building heights, expressed or implied floor lines, window rhythms, and surface materials are the standard variables, and opportunities to develop a dialog between tectonics and environment are typically ignored.

At the other end of the spectrum are buildings in suburban and small town contexts—a significant portion of the American built environment. Although one might expect to find closer interaction between buildings and environment in those settings, where buildings can relate more readily to the ground and in greater harmony with site and surroundings—in turn leading to a more cohesive and aesthetically appealing urban fabric—sterile and/or awkward places are nevertheless the norm. Ironically, it is in suburban and exurban environments, with vast open conditions of territory and setting, that we typically find the worst displays of disposable buildings—those displaying total disrespect for context, serving with impunity a disproportionate interest in cheap imagery, and unapologetic in their servitude to the family car. That some of today's design professionals manage to make meaningful contributions despite current norms and expectations testifies to their commitment and perseverance as well as to the dedication of public officials interested in fostering healthy and attractive urban environments. Those, unfortunately, are not the majority.

So, how do we teach our students about architecture in the surrounding environment? Even the way such a question is phrased indicates how traditionally we think as architects. The building as an icon, a sculptural tour-de-force, and a testament to individual expression—these alluring ideas are difficult to abandon. Even when architects are attuned to site and nature, conflicts emerge when building commissions enforce a mandatory kit of parts regarding spatial organization, forms, and systems, to say nothing of dictated access, parking, materials, and signage, among other factors. Despite those difficulties, however, we believe that it is possible to design in a way that respects the existing conditions of each site and promotes the integration of built and natural systems. The academy bears responsibility for endowing students with appropriate values and encouraging them to challenge the status quo. In short, educators would do well to prepare students to visualize the world as environment + built form rather than as architecture in the landscape or vice versa.

A Few Lessons from the Past

While an integrative approach melding environment and built form may seem cutting edge today, an examination of design history reveals that architecture and the environment have not always been conceptually disconnected. Prehistoric and ancient cultures generally lived lightly on the land and built in a way that reveals a strong understanding of the landscape as well as of climatic and seasonal cycles. Such sophisticated tracking of the ebb and flow of natural cycles made agriculture possible, and—out of intelligence as much as necessity—environmentally sensitive vernacular building techniques have continued unabated for millennia in many parts of the world. Similar

affinities to place also influenced formal design practices at various moments in history. That was particularly true in the United States during the nineteenth-century, when landscape architecture emerged as a profession to help plan for the movement of American civilization across the continent. After the Civil War, thousands of square miles of forest and prairie were converted to fields and cities.

Although modern perspectives on ecology were unknown at that time, the spectacle of rapid change in the landscape compelled many in American society to consider appropriate ways of linking buildings and communities to place. Ralph Waldo Emerson (1803-1882), the nation's preeminent transcendentalist philosopher and poet, envisioned an organic aesthetic through which built form could be inextricably connected to the essential rightness of place. Frederick Law Olmsted (1822-1903), Horace Cleveland (1814-1900), and other pioneer landscape architects translated that theoretical perspective into designed communities, parks, and park systems. Those efforts often involved a close collaboration with architects who shared a similar vision about linking built works to place. That intense awareness of landscape form and function waned during the early years of the twentieth century but was revived after World War II, when modern ecological science was accepted as a necessary informant to reasoned landscape design. Ian McHarg (1920-2001) introduced environmental systems planning to landscape architecture through *Design with Nature*, first published in 1969. Also around that time, architects sought to reconnect with nature in a similar manner through strategies ranging from earth shelter construction techniques to solar collection and super insulation.

The postmodern era has offered both challenges to and new perspectives on that environmental ethic. As approaches to design, postmodern ideologies such as deconstruction, semiotics, and minimalism have certainly contributed to the cult of the architect and landscape architect as solitary genius, yet the postmodern perspective in science has led to a new integrative ecology that includes humans as part of the equation. The new ecology is also allied with emerging perspectives on sustainability and green architecture.

Figure 3. Site vegetation study.

Figure 4. Site suitability study.

Figure 5. Site habitat study.

Upland
Ridge
Riparian
Mixed Pines and Hardwoods

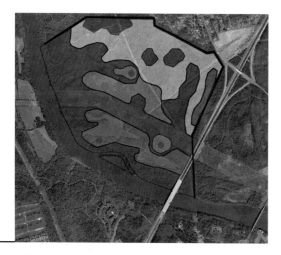

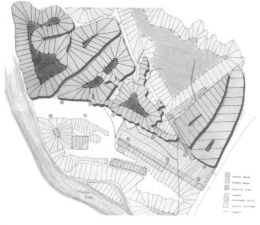

A Master Plan Project

The idea of sustainable community design as it relates to the new ecology served as a major impetus in the organization of the York County project and related studios. The Culture and Heritage Commission of York County had commissioned a plan for a new Museum for Life and the Environment, to be located north of Rock Hill, South Carolina, near the crossing of the Catawba River and Interstate 77. Although the entire site comprises just over 400 acres, the museum setting occupied only about ten percent of that area and was located along the river. The design of that portion was realized through a collaborative of William McDonough + Partners, architecture and community design; Ralph Applebaum Associates, exhibit design; and Warren Byrd and Susan Nelson, landscape architects.

Linkages to the natural systems of the landscape were foregrounded in the museum design both in terms of the fit to place and as opportunities for interpreting the interface of nature and culture. The clients wished that the same environmental sensitivity would inform a community design on the remaining portion of the site. With that goal in mind, the Culture and Heritage Commission turned to the architecture program at University of North Carolina Charlotte and the architecture, landscape architecture, and planning programs at Clemson University. The collaboration between the two universities made sense because, although the site is in South Carolina, it is also part of the larger Charlotte Metropolitan Region.

Clemson's planning students pulled together an extensive regional analysis that provided information about context for the project and offered a large-scale environmental assessment as an informant to a greater understanding of site ecology. **[Fig. 3]** The environmental conditions of the site were explored in considerable depth by Clemson architecture and landscape architecture students, who examined soils, hydrology, vegetation, and many other natural factors and applied the now traditional overlay techniques developed decades earlier by Ian McHarg and others. **[Fig. 4]** They also embraced recently developed principles of landscape ecology by performing a biological analysis, exploring variable habitat conditions, and studying a full array of existing forest conditions on and off the site. Watershed issues were particularly significant given the poor quality of the Catawba River. **[Fig. 5]**

Although sustainability has become an overused term, it is nevertheless a hallmark concept for the new ecology, which considers the role of humans as an essential part of the equation. Reflecting that idea, students also engaged in an extensive cultural analysis. Historical features, a prominent power line corridor, archeological sites, views and vistas, agricultural remnants, and other aspects were studied. The investigation revealed that the site was regionally connected and significant. Students noted that important regional historical themes were manifest on the site. For example: the Catawba tribe left behind artifacts now studied by archaeologists; gold mining pits testify to an early gold rush in the area and a historic quarry is located on one edge of the site.

In layering all of the information about natural and cultural factors, students discovered that two significant ravine areas were of vital importance to the overall ecological health of the site. Based on those findings, they were able to suggest a range of alternative approaches, from developing much of the site at lower density to engaging a small area at higher density. All of the master plans proposed by the students reflected great sensitivity to the existing conditions of site. To varying degrees, all of them also offered visions for sustainable communities in keeping with principles of the new ecology and the basic values of the commission. In every case, students envisioned a development large enough to be economically viable while still clearly respecting and enhancing the existing conditions.

Two of the master plans highlight the range of the proposals and offer alternative perspectives on how environment might inform the structure of a community and the character of its architecture. In a design entitled "Village in the Woods," three students developed a portion of the site more heavily nearest the highway interchange and developed the remainder of the site lightly, with direct ties to the mission of the museum. **[Fig. 6]** The architecture proposed for the latter area echoed the museum's example as green building. In that portion of the site, students suggested solar collection, rainwater collection, the use of a living machine, the use of local and recycled materials, and a clear fit to site topography and hydrology. Environmental interpretation was also considered important; to reflect that priority, the students included a learning center, research facility, and residential lodge. The more densely developed portion of the community was laid out to maximize solar orientation, but it also enhanced human ecology by maximizing walkability and by integrating natural features into all parts of the design. **[Fig. 7]**

At the other end of the spectrum, a different group worked with the grid and other traditional urban forms in a master plan entitled "Catawba Crossing." Those students noted that the grid, a powerful human form dating back to the Ancient Greeks, promotes gathering, neighboring and other interaction, and walkability. Also aware that the grid has been associated with extensive environmental damage, the students sought to prove that it could be adapted to this site in a respectful

Figure 6. "Village in the Woods" master plan.

Figure 7. Site design detail—enhancing human ecology.

and interesting way. Their solution placed a high-density commercial and mixed use area near to the highway and fit residential blocks on the other side of a natural ravine. Not only did the gridded neighborhood flex to meet the existing natural features of the site, but the latter were brought into the community at all levels.

Coda

In pursuing this project, the students came to understand their individual creativity in a much different way. Like writing a sonnet, students had to fit their creative expression into a framework, in this case established by the client, the complexity of the site, and an overriding environmental ethic. In the end, those creative solutions were better because they were grounded. As Emerson might have said, they fit the "essential rightness" of place.

The collaborative studio coincided with a mandated university-wide zero-based curriculum review. The School of Architecture and the Department of Planning and Landscape Architecture were thus encouraged to imagine how their fruitful collaboration in the York County Studio might better inform the curricula and future partnering. Based on those reflections, it was decided that future collaboration to enhance a fuller integration of architecture, landscape, and planning would be institutionalized. For example, a third-year urban design studio will be offered annually to students in all three fields. Furthermore, building on Clemson's long and solid reputation in the architecture of health, the engagement of healthy environments—including natural systems at a broad scale—will be fully developed through collaboration. Those and other efforts will benefit all participating students in a quest to better understand the full potential of melding environment and built form.

Figure 9. Site design detail—flexible grids.

NOTES

1 _ Jane Kay Holtz, *Asphalt Nation: How the Automobile Took Over American Life and How We Can Take It Back* (Berkeley: University of California, 1997).

2 _ Christian Norber-Schulz, *The Concept of Dwelling: On the Way to Figurative Architecture* (New York: Rizzoli International Publications, 1985).

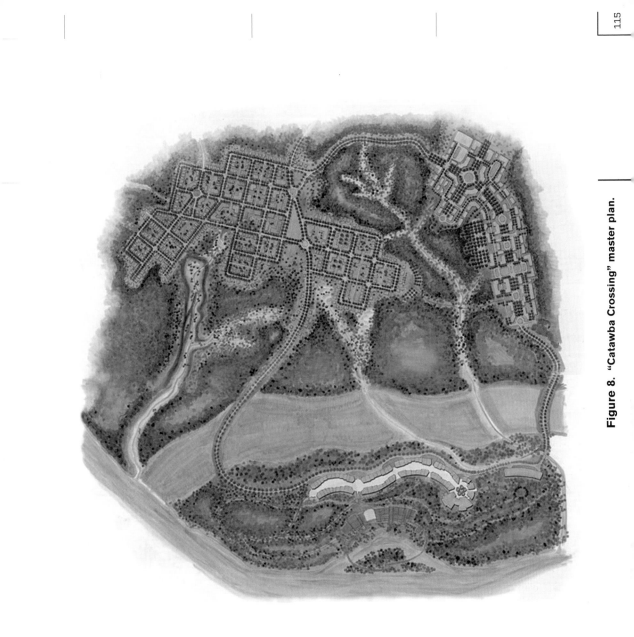

José Cabán, *MCD*, **Robert Hewitt**, *MLA, MCP, and* **Daniel Nadenicek**, *MLA, MS, all teach at Clemson University. Cabán is Chair of the School of Architecture. Nadenicek is Chair of the Department of Planning and Landscape Architecture and Hewitt is an Assistant Professor in the Department of Planning and Landscape Architecture.*

Figure 8. "Catawba Crossing" master plan.

Figure 1

THE MIAMI UNIVERSITY GRADUATE FALLINGWATER STUDIO: EXPLORING THE DUALITY OF LANDSCAPE + ARCHITECTURE

Kimberly Hill and John Reynolds

Our premise for the Graduate Fallingwater Studio, first taught at Miami University in Spring 2004, is that a duality exists between architecture and landscape. Our inquiry positions the designed landscape as architectural space and explores the process of how to conduct the translation of architecture as landscape. Through creative and rigorous site analysis exercises focusing on the relationships of form and space, inside/outside, sequence and movement, physical/dimensional variables, and perception, we aim to discover the relational aspects of site which we refer to as *site DNA*. This DNA is comprised of the fundamental physical and psychological characteristics of site which influence the essence of experience; it is, therefore, the carrier of the relationships between landscape and architecture. The abstract relationships of this site DNA are brought forth through exercises in emotive drawing exploration, speculative construction, and tectonic exploration that serve as the backbone of this studio design process directed towards the discovery, clarification and extension of more concrete site relationships, or DNA.

This first-year, spring term, graduate studio explores the design and construction of environment. What is environment? How do we understand it? How do we react to it? Fallingwater (1935-38), designed by Frank Lloyd Wright, serves as our laboratory for the discovery, explo-

Figure 2

ration, and extension of site DNA relationships through which one can comprehend and communicate the essence of architectural space. The studio has the dual charge of designing a site-specific interior environment—a furniture environment for the Servant's Sitting Room—and a series of pavilions along the walking trails on the Lands of Fallingwater to reveal site context and extend the ecological mission of the Western Pennsylvania Conservancy.[1] With the pretext that furniture is to room as building is to site, the orientation of the studio has continually stressed the process of absorption in order to react with sensitivity to site relationships, and ultimately design, in considering the issues of the construction of environment. Those questions consumed Wright during the journey through which he formulated the Prairie Style. To develop responses to them requires a patience, diligence, and stillness that is often difficult to grasp in our contemporary context.

The traditional means of understanding site—scientific mensuration and spatial calculation—provide only an abstract representation of site attributes. A complete understanding of site requires that the perceived literal condition be complemented equally by an understanding of the site's ephemeral dimensions. Landscape, as site construction, *breathes* in its sensual tactility. Architecture as Landscape shares in that sensibility. Fallingwater embraces the inescapable power of landscape in its dualism of architecture as landscape. Therefore, to distill the site ideation, or DNA, that transforms architecture into landscape, we begin by asking how one addresses the *sensual* in the understanding of landscape and the experience of architecture. Our methodology is to focus the studio on the exploration of landscape experience—beginning with personal narratives and conceptions of wilderness—in an attempt to uncover the site narrative as it relates to life, place, and the sensuality of the situation.

In order to address an often commonplace, detached way of operating in the world as it relates to design process, our exercises are aimed at revealing alternative ways of seeing and thinking about environment. Students journey through a series of short, abstract exercises designed to increase their awareness and sensitivity to landscape via the illustration and affirmation of their inner selves through journaling, poetry, and a variety of graphic media. Linking personal narrative with site experience, these exercises serve to illuminate a process of site interpretation that can be directed abstractly towards a distillation of the site DNA relationships. Each exercise inherently encourages students to connect their personal narrative with the sensual content of site, to discover truth in and through their highly personal responses. Throughout the abstracted development of the creative process, students are further encouraged to explore, maintain, and extend their ideation of landscape in terms of site DNA.

Over the course of the studio, students respond to these exercises in a developing continuum that takes them from confusion to clarity and, consequently, confidence. As a result, we have seen students learn to engage their design process with a candid openness to abstract exploration that carries through into group dynamics. We have oscillated the explorative/interpretive process between individual and collective engagement. Layers of understanding develop from the initial personal reactions, and new ways of seeing and communicating regularly emerge when the students work actively with each other in teams. Through these constantly varying social and tectonic layers, they advance their design work further, in some cases to radical transformation, as if in a completely different time and place. Different colors, textures, scales, and mark making filtered through personal lenses changes the group discussion, resulting in transformed perspective as the students shift their personhood, releasing their individual preconceptions of themselves, architecture, and landscape. Acceptance of the other, or non-controlled, leads to a rawness, or *poiesis*, informed by the sensitivity garnered while pursuing site questions through multiple lenses.

Our approach is structured through a methodological progression: from gathering to explorative study and abstract making, culminating in critical dialogue and response. This process can be illustrated through what transpired during our initial visit to Fallingwater in January 2004. We began the studio by gathering in the traditional cognitive research arena, with several weeks of extensive reading pertaining to the intellectual experience of Fallingwater. Our first day at Bear Run hit the students like an overwhelming wave of cognitive shock in the collision between the sensual and intellectual. They were exhausted and speechless in their struggle to comprehend their experience after their first full day of encounter with site, house, staff, and their inner persons. Lectures, tours, woodland paths, bitter cold, the ever-present sound of Bear Run, and encounter with ice and rock collectively constructed a heightened sensitivity to environment. Their field study introduction to the experience of the Fallingwater site had a cold-call-like quality in its unexpected rawness that demanded complete intellectual and sensual immersion. The rugged quality of Landscape to which Wright was responding had the effect of a sublime silencing of the students. **[Fig. 2]**

Figures 3 & 4

The day's excited, playful exuberance had turned to quiet, contemplative stillness. Recognizing that this is prime and fertile ground for a designer's process, we began the explorative study process with the goal of illustrating how students might harness the power of experience towards uncovering site DNA and the creation of environment. The group discussion the first evening was labored with conversation centered on their encounter with the house, considering what became etched in their mind's eye. Contradiction, anomaly, aberration, and the unexpected emerged from these discussions. Students found themselves at a loss to express comprehensively their experience of site and house. To facilitate their analysis and integration of the sensual and the intellectual, they were encouraged to play through a series of interpretive exercises. Thus began the abstract making part of the process. Their task was to draw gestural studies on large format paper, focusing on their emotional experiences. Students were encouraged to draw with their bodies and take risks with new media for thirty-minute intervals. The focus emphasized the attempt to capture dramatic spatial transitions in mass and void, inside/outside, and sequential, movement-based relationships. We encouraged them to express the tactile and palpable in their drawings with emphasis on the relationship of space to the body. **[Figs. 3 & 4]**

During these activities, students worked furiously in their own world—the realm of personal narrative—in complete engagement with the task at hand and unaware of time. They made rapid emissions of thoughts, feelings, and personal statements. The intensity of their mark-making was the result of corporeal, emotional, and physical immersion as they became covered in their media. Together, they created an *environment*: the landscape of the room that was alive with music, the smoke and popping of the fire, charcoal dust and the smell of paint, with a distinct, intensely cre-

ative energy permeating the room. The previous quietness had been replaced by frenzied, carefree *making* in the spirit of abstract creativity. We then shared not only our own work but our perceptions of work by others in the critique stage, abstracting discussion into a creative experience that served to illuminate lenses of perception, while exploring layers of understanding that elicited aspects of site DNA.

This studio design process was extended across multiple scales, design programs and social constructions. In the phase following the initial drawing exercise, students used their drawings to create a collage that began to distill their conception of the site DNA. The understanding of site derived from the collages served to prompt preliminary furniture design proposals. Upon our return from Fallingwater, students worked to further comprehend the connection of architecture and landscape, object and site through the conception of a *Chinese Wedding Chest*[2] design process problem—an object whose function was to reveal the site relationships at Fallingwater through tectonic expression. The object's construction and details gave material form to site DNA and characteristically expressed the marriage or union of architecture and landscape. This study served to inform the continued development of individual furniture proposals begun at Fallingwater. Following a critique with members of the Fallingwater Administration, students were re-engaged with emotive drawing in a collaborative drawing exercise that established three design teams on the basis of shared DNA ideologies. Collaborative furniture proposals were then developed in a *Team DNA* organizational structure. **[Fig. 1]**

In the collaborative studio phase, design teams worked extremely well together and were highly productive based on shared values and the unique contributions of each individual. During a second visit to Fallingwater in March 2004, the three groups coalesced towards the development of a single furniture proposal distilled during reviews with administration, staff and collective reflection. During this second visit, we began the design process for the Lands of Fallingwater pavilions. Three sites were selected and the student teams were engaged in emotive drawing to begin a continuing tectonic site interpretation exercise in which the site DNA relationships discovered in the earlier design process and furniture design activity congealed with the specific content of each pavilion site, extending the site DNA codes from drawing to object, to furniture, and finally to the pavilion, while respecting the nuance of site, program and situation. At the conclusion of the semester, students presented a single, collaborative furniture proposal along with team proposals for each of the three pavilion sites. **[Figs. 5 & 6]**

This methodology for working in the studio presents an alternative to a world increasingly shaped by the forces of cybernetics, virtual reality and digital mediation. While we do not disregard the role these forces play in the making of the landscape and architecture, we argue that the design process elucidated here affords opportunities for intertwining the personal narratives of the maker with the site codes or DNA. This reciprocity between maker and site is mirrored in the design duality that arises between landscape and architecture, blurring their traditionally constructed professional boundaries and academic terrains. Identifying, exploring, and manifesting site DNA relationships tectonically throughout the design process at a multiplicity of scales and in the context of a variety of programs can lead toward a poiesis of place." Grounded in the situation, expressing the process of making and revealing the identity of the maker with site memory and experience, we anticipate that this design method can foster an increased sensitivity to the design process and its resulting artifacts, leading us, in small steps, on a path to a more humane world.

NOTES

1 _ The Lands of Fallingwater are roughly 1400 acres adjacent to and including the Kaufman family residential property. The Lands have been owned and managed since 1963 by the Western Pennsylvania Conservancy, a public trust, which owns and manages Fallingwater itself.

2 _ The Chinese Wedding Chest problem explored the expression of union, challenging students to reveal the essence of Fallingwater through *making* at the scale of the object, using the joint to express the connection between building and site.

Kimberly Hill, *MLA (Harvard), Assistant Professor and Coordinator of Landscape Studies, and* **John Reynolds**, *M.Arch. (University of Virginia), Associate Professor and Director of Graduate Studies, both teach in the Department of Architecture and Interior Design at Miami University.*

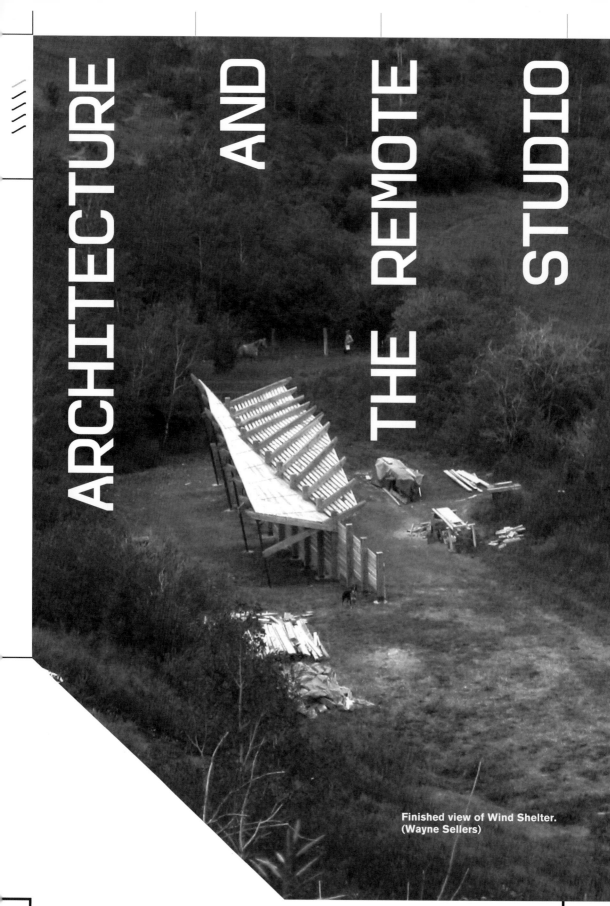

ARCHITECTURE AND THE REMOTE STUDIO

Finished view of Wind Shelter.
(Wayne Sellers)

AN OVERVIEW
Lori Ryker

The practice of architecture is woven into the fabric of our culture, constantly shaping the world in which we live. In recognizing this, we must also recognize that the way in which we educate architects will consequently affect the condition of the built and natural environment. In the Northern Rockies, one of the last regions in the United States to be fully developed and physically transformed, we stand at an impasse of choice. Will we continue to build our cities as they have been built before; will we exploit our resources here as they have been exploited elsewhere; will we forfeit our cultural heritage for the sake of commercial development; will we sacrifice the natural beauty of the mountains, plains, rivers, and lakes for our own perceived needs? Our choices reflect our values. They are not only evident in our day-to-day lives but are codified in our educational programs. Two questions must be considered and responded to not only here in the West, but everywhere. What qualities do we wish for our world? What knowledge do we find essential to impart upon the individuals who will be responsible for creating the world in which we will live? The Remote Studio is one possibility for addressing these questions.

The development of the Remote Studio grew out of my own educational experience. In the early 1990s, I completed a Master of Architecture degree at Harvard's Graduate School of Design. For most of us, the thesis project embodied the

A VIEW FROM WITHIN
Justin Smith

The appeal of the Remote Studio Course for many of the participating students, including me, was a summer spent outside in southwest Montana, as opposed to a semester in the design studios. We were committed to spending the time outdoors, learning about the region, and debating environmental philosophy, but Lori also developed a program that helped shape the way we look at architecture and its design process. I distinctly remember how the meetings throughout spring semester progressed: There was discussion about the organization of the program and worry about tuition and course credit. Eventually, those concerns were balanced by questions about how many hikes we would go on and where we would go backpacking, making sure that we could spend sufficient time outside. Over seven weeks, the studio's activities took place in and around beautiful Paradise Valley, south of Livingston, Montana. The Remote Studio promised to provide us with wild experiences. Most of us feel as Aldo Leopold did, that "there are some who can live without wild things, and some who cannot." The Remote Studio is a program developed by, and for, those who cannot.

In exchange for cleaning up ten years of dirt and repairing broken windows, Mr. O'Hair let us stay in the abandoned Richland Schoolhouse, situated on his ranch, about fifteen minutes south of Livingston. A week before the course began, we

First group overnight trip up the West Boulder River. (Lori Ryker)

Students negotiating a West Boulder River crossing. (Wayne Sellers)

LR ///// culmination of our thinking, a test of our potential, a quest for theorizing and practicing our beliefs. My work focused on the relationship of landscape and place to architecture. As the design work developed, a thesis advisor pointed out to me that there was a shared attribute to the sites I chose to work with: all were disturbed landscapes in one way or another. Recognizing the disturbed landscapes in which we live became the first of many lessons concerning the perception and understanding of nature and culture.

Years later I was driving through Wyoming, a vast place that requires close-up study for its full appreciation. Watching the grass roll out along the horizon as I moved through it, I wondered, what is it about the landscape that resonates within us, and why is it that schools of architecture spend so much time focused on the object of architecture as precedent and idea of creation rather than the natural world itself?

The Ph.D. program at Texas A&M University provided a later opportunity for me to explore this question further along with others. The upshot of my dissertation, the Remote Studio, is profiled here, while my practice with Ryker/Nave Design and RN Construction focus on the professional practice of these ideas. Practice is a humbling act, making reality of academic dreams, while teaching supports visionary interests. They are all bound together by a love of nature, landscape, and the

JS ///// spent a dirty weekend cleaning the schoolhouse, and before long we established it as a worthy place of residence to call home for the seven weeks of the program.

Initially, our focus was on seeing and being a part of the beautiful outdoors. This was especially easy given our direct view across Paradise Valley to the Absaroka Mountains. Our community room/studio/kitchen, where we spent most of our indoor time, had enormous picture windows facing directly east. At any point during the day, if we became even slightly confused as to what we were working on and why, it took only a glimpse outside to remind us. Each morning, breakfast was consumed as the sun crawled up from behind the Absorakas; days were spent beyond the walls of the schoolhouse; and, as the last hint of color disappeared from the sky over Paradise Valley, we devoured our home-cooked gourmet meals. Our first excursion into the wilderness was a daylong loop trip in the Absaroka Mountains that was strenuous but extremely worthwhile. The hike allowed us to expend some extra energy and gave us time for personal reflection. We were also able to glimpse the beautiful valley from above as well as some spectacular views of the Absaroka Mountains beyond.

Much of the first few weeks of the program were also spent extensively exploring the North Star Ranch, the site for the design and build

Patty Flores's vessel project on the North Star Ranch. (Patty Flores)

Steve Harrop's vessel project on the North Star Ranch. (Steve Harrop)

LR ///// search for being of a particular place.

Aristotle claimed that wisdom arises from the experiences of adventure and leisure. Adventure provides first hand experiences contributing to who we become, whereas leisure provides time for contemplation and eventually wisdom gained through the assimilation of multiple experiences. The Remote Studio, which draws upon Aristotle's idea, is developed as a semester long immersion in the wild lands of Montana for students of architecture who are interested in exploring the relation of place to architecture, understanding better the holistic approach to an ecological architecture, and learning about their own creative intuition and its ties to direct experiences in the world.

The Program, begun in 1997 while teaching at Texas A&M, currently runs through Montana State University's School of Architecture and takes place off-campus in a live and learn environment within the Yellowstone eco-region, most recently an old school house. Ten students are enrolled in a full semester of coursework that includes design studio, advanced environmental theory, and individual problems of construction, all of which I teach. The courses are woven together with lessons in theory and first-hand experiences, providing an in-depth exploration of the surrounding environment and culture.

Readings and discussions of ecology, environmental philosophy, place, and phenomenology

JS ///// project. The first assignment was a series of "vessel" projects each of us was to construct. The vessels were to convey our ideas or beliefs about the region or the ranch, and, on a small scale, they let us interpret those ideas in connection with our own beliefs about the environment and our effect upon it. While the first vessels were portable, the final vessel we each constructed was built in place on the North Star Ranch as a reference to and of the permanence of the area and the temporary contact we shared with it. Understanding the intimate relationship between the natural landscape and the man-made landscape of our architecture was an important focus of the studio.

In addition to the hikes and vessel projects, we met with both the owner and the manager of the North Star Ranch in order to develop an understanding of their aspirations for the project, which was a wind shelter to serve a small valley pasture on the ranch, protecting horses from frequent storms in the winter and providing shade in the summer. We were limited to a six-week period for design and construction. We quickly started developing a proposal. Fortunately, the schoolhouse provided us with one of the best tools for design: wall to wall chalkboards in all three rooms. These chalkboards functioned exceptionally well as a backdrop for our design charrettes, and left traces of ten students'

Setting shelter posts on a rainy June day. (Wayne Sellers)

Typical rigorous day of construction. (Lori Ryker)

Setting rafters for wind shelter. (Wayne Sellers)

Finished view of Wind Shelter. (Wayne Sellers)

LR ///// serve as the framework from which students begin to explore their design projects, while backcountry experiences bring them to a time of personal testing, contemplation, and comprehension. A series of "vessels" built from local materials allow for development and expression of an individual's creativity grown out of their experiences of a particular place. The group design/build project takes their lessons to a practical level, integrating theory, experience, and creativity into the making of architecture. Each design/build project is selected for its ability to serve a client, expand the general public's experience of architecture, and act as an intermediary experience from developed environments to wild and natural environments such as the Absaroka-Beartooth Wilderness.

For the design/build project, students take responsibility for communicating with a client, developing a proposal, negotiating its appropriateness, developing details, material palette, cost, and production. Discussions of responsibility and appropriateness to place, landscape, and resource remain constants during this period. Students learn how to work with one another, communicate ideas, and speak up for what they believe. Building is a test not only of physical endurance but also of performing as a group in order to make something that supports a developing ethic. The completion of the project brings the Remote Studio experience to its end. Whereas some may only recognize the value of the practical experience of construction and client relations, I see

JS ///// thoughts strewn across the walls, constantly reminding us of the project's evolution. The first proposal for the shelter slightly misinterpreted the goals of the client, and a second attempt was necessary. The final result not only solved the client's problem but also resulted in a much more graceful design solution. The functional "key" to the proposal was a gate incorporated into the scheme to allow a smaller portion of the pasture to be closed off. This gate provided separation between pastures while retaining the close proximity of new and old horses, a common concern in introducing new horses to the ranch. The vertical spacing of the wood clad wall opened the structure to a gentle flow of air, light, and views. The result of our proposal is a piece of architecture that flows out of the valley, picking up the smooth rolling texture of the meadow and providing a delicately balanced roof to shelter the horses.

With the client's approval, we started the hands-on phase: material selection, cost estimation, detail drawing, digging, cutting, drilling, and connecting the shelter to its pasture. In a chaotic maelstrom of events, the last three weeks of the program consisted mainly of building with a rapid learning curve for all of those not proficient in the art of construction or carpentry. The initial struggle was to refine a system for load transfer that was both cost effective and appropriate to our design. We solved this necessity by incorporating steel into the wooden structure, thereby providing the stiffness to resist significant Montana wind

LR ///// these lessons as a necessity for learning more about the self, gaining a sense of responsibility toward the world, landscape, and architecture, which in-turn provides young architects confidence to practice what they believe.

Lori Ryker, *M.Arch., Ph.D., is an Assistant Professor in the School of Architecture at Montana State University.*

Shadow patterns cast on open gate showing roof and wall details. (Wayne Sellers)

forces. Shop drawings for the steel were quickly
JS ///// developed and given to the local welding shop for fabrication. Engaging with the local steel fabricator and lumber mill provided us with a great opportunity to work with custom materials and details. With only three short weeks for construction, our schedule was often dictated by what materials were readily available at the fabricator or mill. Sometimes, a wait for materials gave us the excuse for another outdoor adventure.

Living in a small schoolhouse and sweating out a project together allowed the eleven of us to developed a significant bond. We developed our own small community within the larger community of southwest Montana. As with any community, we had occasional disputes and miscommunications, but each provided us with new insight into how a community works. The course helped us recognize the interplay between ranching, the town, and the glorious environment that sustains the life of the area. The design of the project evolved as a response to that place as we became aware of it over the course of the summer. The lessons learned from the hands-on experience, from our community and our client, were more beneficial than those received in our previous four years at school. From this experience we each developed a new interpretation of the design process, its role in architecture, and the factors critical to environmentally sensitive and responsible design.

REMOTE STUDIO STUDENTS, 2003

Patty Flores
Cindy Freier
Nick Fulton
Brian Gregoire
Steve Harrop
Andrea Kauffman
Joe Roodell
Wayne Sellers
Justin Smith
Eva Unruh

Justin Smith *received his M.Arch. in May 2004 from the School of Architecture at Montana State University.*

**Entering *Double Negative*,
Mormon Mesa, Nevada,
1 Oct. 2002.**

LESSONS FOR ARCHITECTURE: LAND ARTS OF THE AMERICAN WEST

Chris Taylor

"*It is hard to believe the amount of fine sand in my tent right now. The screen ceiling only lets in the fines, so there is a nice fine layer over everything. I suppose I should have zipped up the ceiling and vent panels last night—they are closed now. This morning began with an assessment of the situation with the wind and student's ability to work here. We made the call to hold and reconsider at noon. The morning seemed productive for most and the wind held back a bit. So we decided to stay. It was manageable (strong but not overwhelming) all day. Around dinner the gusts started again and then changed after dark to come out of the north—the temperature dropped considerably.*"

(8:55pm 17 Sep. 2003, Muley Point, Utah)

"*This morning began with a cold start, huddled around a fire that kept everyone close. The wind parted after another night of firm blowing, the air crisp and much clearer. The buttes of Monument Valley jumped out of the view without their blanket of haze. Spirits seemed to improve with the shift in weather. There are still a few struggling, but most have jumped in and are making, or are at least active. Looking forward to the conversation tomorrow about the work, both to hear what people have been up to, and also to learn about the ideas developing.*"

(10:00pm 18 Sep. 2003, Muley Point, Utah)

Bonneville Dike across Bonneville Salt Flat, Utah, 8 Sept, 2003.

(Students overlooking the Goosenecks and Monument Valley, Muley Point, Utah, 18 Sep. 2003.

Spiral Jetty detail, Promontory Point, Great Salt Lake, Utah, 12 Sep. 2003.

Moonhouse, Cedar Mesa, Utah, 19 Sep. 2003.

Fence across playa, Bonneville Salt Flat, Utah, 8 Sep. 2003.

LAND ARTS OF THE AMERICAN WEST is a studio-based, field study program that investigates land arts from pre-contact Native American to contemporary Euro-American cultures. It is a program that views land as a continuum across time and cultures, a program that demonstrates the potential of situating questions between disciplines and definitions, between landscape and architecture. Land Arts practices can include everything from constructing a road, to taking a walk, building a monument, or leaving a mark in the sand. We learn from the fact that Donald Judd surrounded himself with both contemporary sculpture and Navajo rugs, that *Chaco Canyon* and *Roden Crater* function as celestial instruments, and that the *Very Large Array* is a scientific research center with a powerful aesthetic presence on the land.

LAND ARTS is a collaboration between Studio Art at the University of New Mexico and Design at the University of Texas at Austin. Fourteen students and two faculty spend a semester living and working in the southwestern landscape with guest scholars in disciplines including archeology, art history, architecture, ceramics, criticism, writing, design, and studio art. Occupying the land for weeks at a time, living as a nomadic group and working directly in the environment, students navigate issues of culture, site, community, and self. The students develop skills of perception and analysis unattainable in a standard classroom setting. **LAND ARTS** is an interdisciplinary model of education that hinges on the relation between human interventions and the landscape.

LAND ARTS is like a study abroad program in our own backyard. We venture into territory unknown to most and learn to experience this world anew. Exposed to new cultures, languages, and customs, we also take in the land from a different perspective. For many of us, the trip into the arid regions of the West is a journey into a place with different rules, boundaries, and structures than home. The desert offers a possibility; it is a legible landscape where we can learn to read perhaps more easily than we can in the green meadows and forests of wetter climates. The absence of water, its preciousness, contains valuable lessons.

After five weeks living (camping) and working on the land, students were equipped with new sensibilities upon entering *Double Negative*, Michael Heizer's seminal earthwork cut into Mormon Mesa, Nevada, in 1969. The piece was no longer the isolated act of one man, but a complex set of relations, forces, and scales. These included signs of habitation and intervention within the work that ranged from the nests of small birds and animals to beer bottles, shell casings, and an old fire ring. The erosion of the original excavation was also telling. It revealed the strength and

weakness of the geology of the site. No longer mere visual patterns in a surface, the soft areas had given way, taken over by the wind and rain. Boulders settled and sand drifts swelled through the bottom of the cut. Rather than reading as a monumental intrusion on the land, for this group of students, *Double Negative* seemed delicate and downright small in comparison with the size of the mesa it occupies, overlooking the Virgin Valley and mountains beyond. In fact, we were sheltered from the strong winds and intense afternoon heat by this sculpture that is as long as the Empire State Building is tall.

LAND ARTS begins with a question rooted in the practices of making art and expands through design to architecture. It is the interdisciplinary nature of the inquiry that becomes fruitful, connecting the visual language of art and design to the physical language of the land and its use. The very fact that we do not apprehend the sites we visit from one definition or bound discipline opens the possibility for new ways to construct an education. The discipline of architecture stands to learn much from this strategy. In the academy and the professional world, it is common to have a project with a distant site known only through photographs or perhaps a brief encounter. A photograph of a site and an experience of place are two radically different things. LAND ARTS teaches us the value of committing to the energy of experi-

ence, of investing time in the subtle reading of site, of understanding a sense of place.

The hike across Cedar Mesa, Utah, from Emigrant Trail to the north edge of Snow Flat brings us through low piñon and juniper cover growing from loose red sand. A narrow trail leads through the fragile cryptobiotic crust that attempts to hold the sand in place. Soon we emerge onto a large sandstone formation that marks the edge of a deep canyon. At the rim, we can see our destination midway up the other side: *Moonhouse*, a ±1200-year-old settlement built of mud and rock into the steep canyon wall. We pause for a minute to wonder if the seasonal creek at the bottom once flowed year round. After a bit of searching, we find the drop-in point and begin the slow climb down into the canyon. The trail fades and reappears with the consistency of the footing; narrow rock shelves give way to loose sand and scruffy vegetation. The trail up the other side, while still steep, is more established. Rounding the corner at the large stone 'thumbs,' we approach a series of structures seamlessly fitted into the canyon wall. Prints left by the hands and feet of the makers, still legible in the surface of the mud, and the remaining painted pictographs on the rock walls collapse a connection across time. We enter the continuum of human intervention with the land.

LAND ARTS hopes to confirm the idea that, by bringing students out into the world instead of

the world into the classroom, we can fundamentally change how we all learn, create, and view our surroundings. In this context, we strive to make deeper and more precise connections within our work and be inspired to create work that makes broader connections outside of ourselves.

Chris Taylor *is an Assistant Professor of Design in the Department of Art and Art History at the University of Texas at Austin. He is also an architect and Co-Director of* Land Arts of the American West.

More information about Land Arts of the American West *can be found online at:* *http://design2.art.utexas.edu/land_arts.*

"Woke today before the sun, around 5:30am. Entered The Lightning Field *just before first light. It was great to spend some time out there before the sun began to warm the sky. Quiet, cool, immense. I walked to the middle of the eastern edge of the field and waited. Watched as the eastern horizon began to glow red. As it turned yellow, the red made its way across the sky to the west, the clouds doing wonders for the sun's rise as they had for it's setting last night. As the light grew in the valley so did the electricity of the poles. They began to gather the light of the sun and start the process of turning white hot, shimmering there before the horizon. It did not last long before the poles accepted the dull sheen from the over-lit day and faded back into the landscape."*

(10:00pm 28 Oct. 2003, Madrid, New Mexico)

Colon by Ryan Henel, Blue Notch, Lake Powell, Utah, 15 Sep. 2003, photography by Ryan Henel.

PARTICIPANTS
Bill Gilbert (UNM co-director), Chris Taylor (UT co-director)

2002
Julie Anand, Jeff Beekman, Joy Davidson, Blake Gibson, Esteban Hinojosa, Adam Hitt, Liz Hunt, Collen Moffet, Carolyn Moore, Jessica Murray, Katie Phillips, Geordie Shepperd, Jane Taylor, and Ryan Thompson.

2003
Katherine Bash, Karessa Bowens, Ledia Carroll, Kate Crowe, Malia Davis, Amanda Douberley, Zach Griffith, Gloria Haag, Ryan Henel, Mary Nakigan, Erika Osbourne, Xochitl Paredes, Gabriel Romero.

SITES
Sites visited include: El Vado Lake, Bisti Badlands, Chaco Canyon, Cebolla Canyon, *The Lightning Field*, *Very Large Array*, Bosque del Apache, Tenabo, in New Mexico; Muley Point, Cedar Mesa, Moonhouse, Goblin Valley, Blue Notch Canyon, Lake Powell, CLUI Wendover, and *Spiral Jetty*, at Promontory Point, Great Salt Lake, Utah; Fire Point, at the North Rim of the Grand Canyon, and *Roden Crater* in Arizona; *Double Negative*, in Overton, Nevada; Boquillas Canyon, and Marfa, in Texas; and Mata Ortiz, in Mexico

GUESTS
LAND ARTS guest scholars have included: Nick Abdalla and Susan Spring, artists;

Tori Arpad, artist; Jerry Brody, art historian and Chaco expert; Matt Coolidge, Director, Center for Land Use Interpretation; William Fox, writer; Hector Gallegos and Graciela Martinez, Mata Ortiz Potters; Mary Lewis Garcia, Acoma Pueblo potter; Lucy Lippard, author and cultural critic; Tom McGrath and Nancy Taylor, Skystone Foundation; Ann Reynolds, art historian and Robert Smithson scholar; Kathleen Shields, DIA Foundation Administrator of *The Lightning Field*; Marianne Stockebrand, Director, Chinati Foundation; Simone Swan, builder and Director of Adobe Alliance; Henry Walt, archeologist and Piro culture expert; Blaine Young, architect and river guide; and Joe Zuni, Isleta Pueblo Elder.

COURSEWORK

LAND ARTS includes four course topic areas. **Site-specific Sculpture** places contemporary site work in the context of a continuous tradition of landscape based art making that is thousands of years old; **Site-specific Shelter** investigates issues of inhabitation, the record of life in the landscape, and asks students to construct, detail, and document site-based interventions; **Indigenous Ceramics** introduces artists and designers to the use of native materials gathered on site to make, decorate, and fire vessels related to the functional and ritual needs of the group; and **Documents: Body, Landscape, Memory** explores the question of mapping within the landscape and the relation of the body to site.

U-TURN STUDIO

Pierre Bélanger

The Manifesto

As a growing delta region spreading along the Maas and the Rhine, Holland is considered the densest country in the world. By 2010, the Dutch want to build close to one million new homes for over one million new families that are migrating from city centers to bulk suburban housing locations around the Deltametropolis. Designed into the Fifth Report on Spatial Planning, these housing projects ironically maintain the contrast between city space and the peri-urban landscape.

This all means one thing: Holland is sprawling. Dutch cities are swelling and will eventually merge into a large cosmopolitan agglomeration of ring roads, highways, and urban communities. At this regional scale, the function of motorways is magnified: they organize, much like horizontal elevators, access and communication to and from different areas for living, working, playing, and moving. How then do we mobilize the present condition of the A13, as well as other motorway-regions, in order to project their future shape?

Using the A4 as a mirror example, this studio illustrates how ten new exits along the spine of the A13 can accomplish this. The exits function just like u-turns: a segment of the highway is deactivated, a dead end is created, and a new region is catalyzed. These exit designs create traffic-based landscapes: off ramps become ware-

Gravitational Pull: Demographic Concentrations across Northern Europe in 2003

Gravitational Pull: Demographic concentrations across Northern Europe in 2003.

Kleinpolderplein: The highway interchange as a bulging three-dimensional landscape.

Pre-Flight Logistics: Suitcases as crates and students as couriers.

houses, verges become bus stations, rest stops become hotels, highways become runways, clover leafs become housing projects, and knots become travel plazas. As an amalgamation of different visions, these new landscapes describe a hybrid automotive infrastructure that curiously suggests a larger question about the future of mobility in the Netherlands: are we designing it or is it designing us?

The Studio

The U-Turn Studio took place in the Faculty of Architecture, Landscape, and Design at the University of Toronto and was exhibited at the Rotterdam Architecture Biennale. The project involved the design of a new highway system between Amsterdam & Rotterdam. The studio format consisted of two trips to the Netherlands and a six-month production period in Canada. For the exhibition, the students produced fifteen design case studies of the A13 motorway-region. The first phase of the project involved research of the A13/A4 case study site in the Netherlands. During the field research, several curious discoveries were made about the Dutch landscape: swelling cellular networks on buildings, massive queues for single-family housing projects, a vast culture of truckers, gambling rings, and illegal speed bike races. Five generic concepts were then formulated to describe the spatial layers of the A13/A4 region by characterizing it as a

traffic-landscape. Each concept dealt respectively with typologies of surface, motorway urbanism, scale of growth, organization of traffic and the architecture of motorways. The second phase of the studio was a response to that research. Design projects were conceived as futuristic investigations of the A13 motorway region. These new traffic-landscapes incorporate the contradictions found between the projected vision of the 2001 Dutch Master Plan and the astonishing reality of what is actually happening on the surface of Dutch urban space.

The U-Turn Studio was the work of eight graduate students at the University of Toronto. Participants came from the disciplines of architecture, landscape architecture, and urban design, with past experiences in medicine, construction, biology, and philosophy. The suitcases and transportation materials were supplied by a French-Chinese luggage company, a Polish logistics group, and an Indian media duplication agency.

Students: Lina Aziz, Vineet Chaudhary, Laragh Halldorson, Selena Kwok, Neil Nacionales, Zhao Pei, Chris Routley, Simon Yue.

Pierre Bélanger, MLA, is an Assistant Professor in the Faculty of Architecture, Landscape, and Design at the University of Toronto.

All photographs are by Piet Mazereeuw.

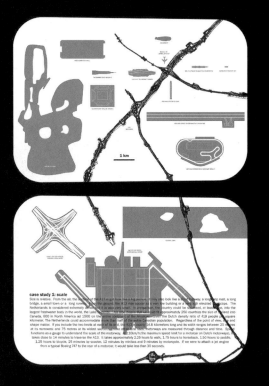

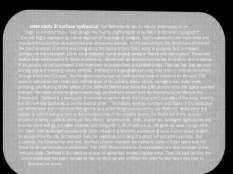

case study 3: surface hydraulics The Netherlands has no natural watersheds as we might understand them. Even though the country might appear to be flat, it is incredibly topographic. It is also highly regulated by a strict regimen of hydrological budgets. Dutch watersheds are engineered and mechanized to function as automated and unmanned designs. In the past century, the Dutch have witnessed the mechanization of almost everything along the food and fuel chain; water is pumped, food is shipped, animals are manufactured, plants are prototyped, fuel is tanked, waste is filtered and shit is piped. Power has shifted from wind to petrol to diesel to electricity. Movement has evolved from horses to boats to cars to planes. If the good is not yet automated, it will eventually be streamlined and prefabricated. They say that they are even cloning pigs and inventing robotic vehicles. Delfland is the geographical entity that refers to a hydraulic system through which the A13 runs. The Hoogheemraadschap van Delfland has been in existence for the past 750 years to administer the control and maintenance of the polders, dikes, canals, storage areas, water levels, pumping, and flushing of the system of the Delfland district ever since the 12th century when the space was first drained. The lands of the Hoogheemraadschap van Delfland extend from the boundaries in the Maas to the Zoetermeer. Delfland is a landscape of cumulative control where the constructed boundary of the water board is the only unit that produces an environmental order. ... The history, ecology, condition and future of the landscape can still be seen and understood through the lens of the Hoogheemraadschap van Delfland. While water has ceased to control and give form to the infrastructures of the modern society, the Dutch are in the unusual situation of being unable to render this history. Governments, cities, municipalities, ecologies, agricultures and estates come and go, but water endures, and along with it, its infrastructure. Life goes on, seen change while the Dutch rural landscape maintains its 18th c. oil-painting likeness: a pleasure ground, a picturesque subject, an escape from the city, but beneath it all, the ceaseless pounding of a silent infrastructure persists. The Zuiderzee, the Deltawerken and now, the River projects maintain the hydraulic parts of Dutch space that will never be left uncontrolled or unplumbed. The 1957 Watersnoodramp (flood disaster) is a sour reminder of the entropic state. Delfland is the machine whose infrastructure evokes obsolescence. Over the past century, the Dutch landscape has been claimed as flat, constructed and artificial; the order for the future may best be described as tonic.

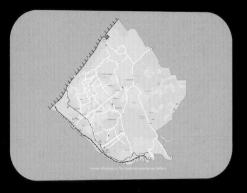

case study 1: scale

Size is relative. From the air, the surface of the A13 might look like a log aluminum trolley, also look like a small highway, a long strip mall, a long bridge, a small town or a long runway toward the ground. the A13 may appear as a very low building or a wide flat elevated landscape. The Netherlands is considered extremely developed; it is also very small. In comparison, the country could be squeezed, at least twice, into the largest freshwater body in the world, the Lake Superior. The land mass that makes up approximately 250 countries the size of Holland into Canada, 600 in North America ad 1500 on the entire continent of the Americas, over the Dutch density ratio of 419 people per square kilometer. The Netherlands could accommodate more than half of the entire Canadian population. Regardless of the point of view, size and shape matter. If you include the two knots at each of its ends, the A13 is about 54.8 kilometers long and its width ranges between 20 metres at its narrowest and 75 metres at its widest section, where the motorways are measured through distance and time. Speed functions as a gauge to understand the scale of the motorway. At 100km/h (the maximum speed limit for a motorcar on Dutch motorways), it takes close to 34 minutes to traverse the A13. It takes approximately 2.25 hours to walk, 1.75 hours to horseback, 1.50 hours to peddle, 1.25 hours to bicycle, 25 minutes by scooter, 12 minutes by minibus and 9 minutes by motorcycle. If we were to attach a jet engine from a typical Boeing 747 to the rear of a motorcar, it would take less than 30 seconds.

Case 2. Scale.

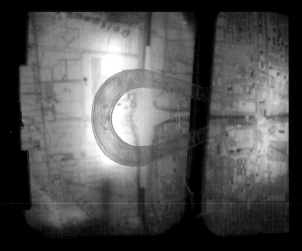

Case 3. Surface Hydraulics .

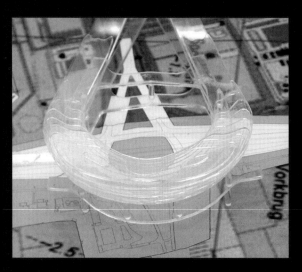

Case 7. U-Turn Car Park: dead ends as live urban configurations.

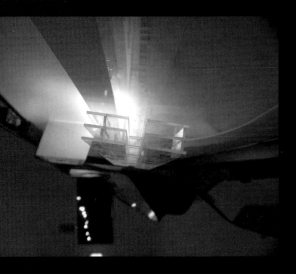

Case 8. Highway Motel: roadsides as 24-hour rest stops.

Case 6. Flyover Truck-Stop: offramps and overpasses as one-stop shop for truckers and travellers.

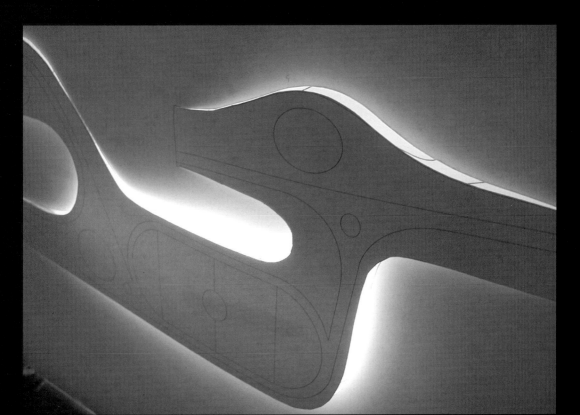

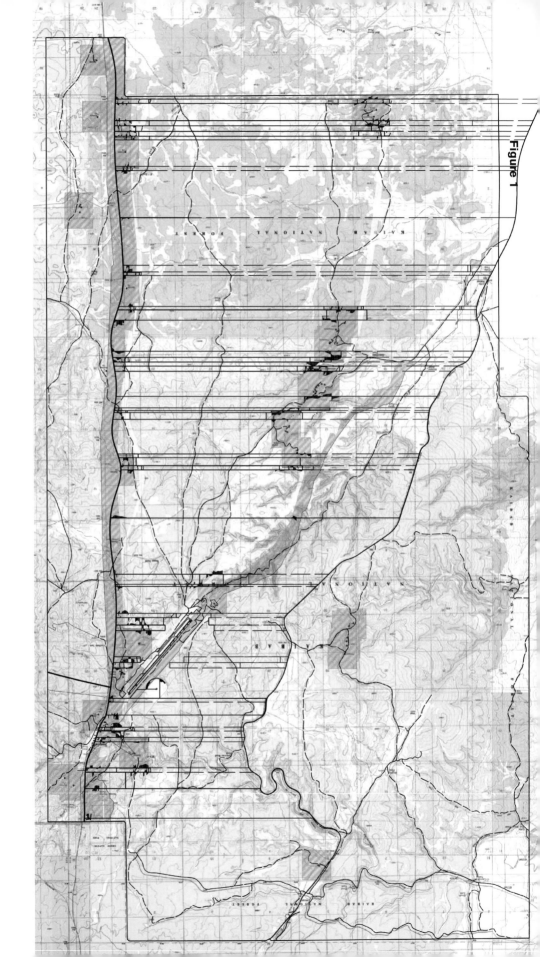

Figure 1

NEGOTIATING THE NATIONAL FORESTS

Claire Johnson

Introduction

Within architecture, there has been a tendency to use reductive explanations for landscape and to assume that contemporary people share a coherent understanding of our relationship to the environment. Many architects assume that the question of our role in landscape has been solved: they argue that landscapes are inevitably artificial and therefore just as legitimately manipulated as architecture, that there is no real boundary between people and the environment, or that questions of how and why we value landscape are simply irrelevant. However, within the United States, debate over the use of public lands suggests that understanding of landscape is anything but coherent. Politics—specifically, the interpretation and implementation of federal legislation regarding public lands—provides insight into the many competing views on people and landscape. Policy offers a messier but less abstract means through which to understand the social meaning of landscape in America. Federally-owned lands have been specially designated as some of the most important landscapes in the country. However, *why* they are important, and what our role in them should be, remains undecided. Federal lands have become a locus for public debate about our relation to landscape in general, and thus provide an opportunity for architects to

Figure 2

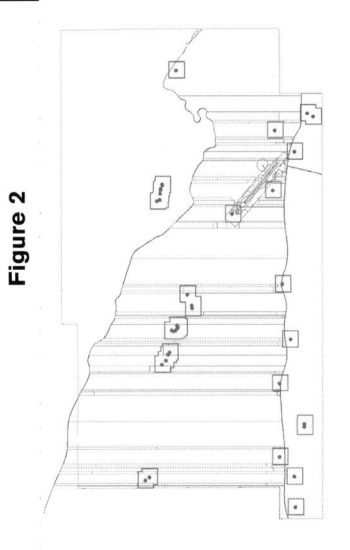

MINES

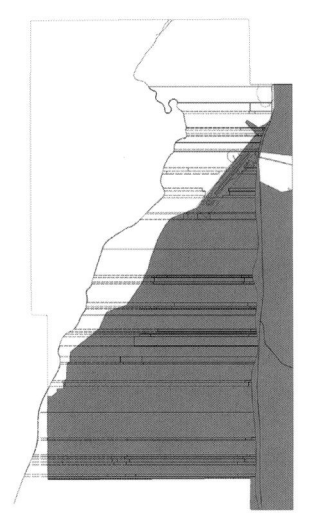

TIMBER SALES

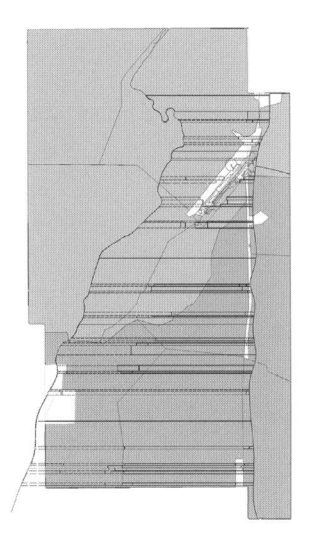

RANGE ALLOTMENTS

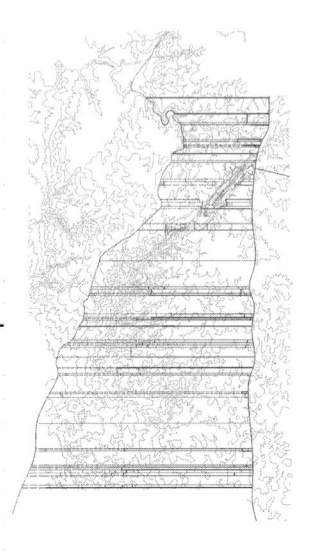

CONTOURS

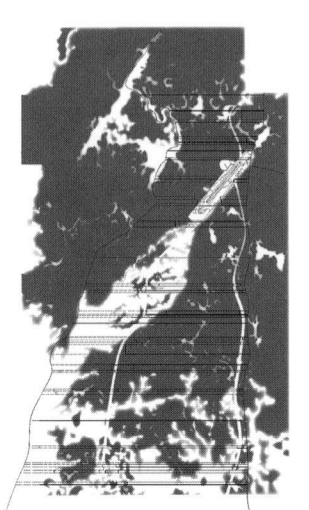

FOREST COVER

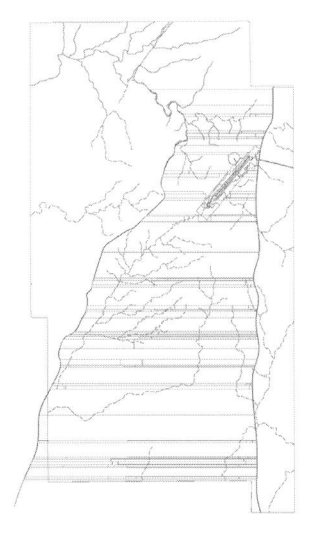

WATER

OVERLAPS

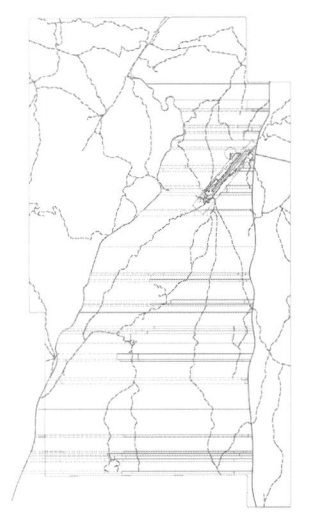

FOREST SERVICE ROADS

get involved in the discussion concerning landscape and, in particular, land politics. *Negotiating the National Forests*, a thesis project carried out at Princeton University in Spring 2003, looks at the wide array of landscape/environmental values people bring to the debate over federal lands and suggests what architecture can do to express those values, affect them, and instigate relevant political change.

Site: Federal Lands

There are three main types of public land in the United States, all defined by legislation and managed by federal agencies. National Parks, established in 1916, are the most familiar type. Set aside for use by visitors, they are generally regarded as scenic or historical sites, the meaning of which is derived from the psychological and/or aesthetic values associated with them in the popular imagination. A second type of public land, the Wilderness Area, was legislated in 1964 and is distinguished by its lack of permanent human presence. These territories come closest to representing the idea of intrinsic value of the environment, and severe restrictions are put on human visitors.

National Forests, instituted in the 1890s, are the oldest public lands in the U.S. and constitute 27% of federally-owned lands. They are governed by a multiple use mandate, which has made them the center of policy debate concerning the proper use of federal lands in general. National Forest legislation, most notably the Multiple Use Sustained Yield Act (MUSY) of 1960, requires that logging, mining, oil exploration, ranching, recreation, wilderness and wildlife preservation, and aesthetic/scenic values be allowed to coexist within each forest. The multiple use concept has been criticized for creating gridlock between conflicting interests in each forest. MUSY requires that various interests be considered but gives no indication of priorities. Local forest managers are given the authority to make decisions, but their judgment is easily assailed and frequently challenged in court. Policy analysts have accused MUSY of arriving at a solution of politics rather than implementation: although the law recognizes all players and their interests, it produces a crisis of public authority in which competing user groups challenge and demonize the National Forest Service. The National Forests are where understandings about the value of land clash most, where a variety of seemingly incompatible programs collide, and where very different user groups confront each other.

Negotiating the National Forests began as a prototype for dealing with the vast territory held by the National Forest Service. The project addresses and exploits the conditions in the National Forests through an architectural intervention within a 327,367-acre portion of Kaibab National Forest, just south of the Grand Canyon in northwestern Arizona. Kaibab's proximity to one of the nation's most famous National Parks allows for play between different notions of the meaning of public lands. The project focuses on an area between two transportation pathways: Highway 64, the only route providing access to and from the main portion of the Grand Canyon, and the Grand Canyon Railroad, a tourist line running into the park. Both of these routes pass through Kaibab, making the forest the threshold to the park.

Possession is Nine-Tenths of the Law

To show how architecture could play a role in land-use politics, the project began by examining existing infrastructure within Kaibab National Forest. Resource-extraction and ranching activities had a physical expression already—mining and logging roads, fences for cattle enclosures, water tanks and catchment basins, among other elements **[Fig. 2]**—whereas recreational and wilderness activities did not. Consequently, it followed that the project should involve the introduction of visitor-related infrastructure. This would give a physical presence to users without an economic stake in the forest, and import a wider range of environmental values, all in keeping with the constituent activities guaranteed by MUSY. Four million visitors a year travel through Kaibab on their way to the Grand Canyon National Park, but the Grand Canyon can only accommodate one million overnight stays per year. The remaining three million potential stays became the audience for this project and began to define the extents of the program.

Tourists in the Forests

This project embraces a series of contradictions: building a physical expression of environmental values without imposing any one discourse; playing legislated multiple use and physical multiple use against each other; and proposing infrastructure that increases tensions between users. It structures an uncertain outcome and sparks policy change rather than installing an infrastructure that reconciles users and remains static.

The fundamental operation of the project is to identify areas within Kaibab National Forest where the legislated boundaries of several user groups overlap and to insert visitors into those already-contested spaces. By intensifying physical proximity, the scheme forces users to confront the full repercussions of multiple use landscapes.

Tourists are drawn into the overlap zones as they seek out visitor services: campsites, visitor centers, hiking trails, restrooms, "event" areas, administrative buildings, ranger housing, and equipment storage. These comprise the typical amenities in the National Parks, altered here in placement and form to reflect the situation in the National Forests. To access these services, a series of parallel, straight roads penetrate the site, leading westward from Highway 64. These access roads contrast strongly with the picturesque routes typically designed in the National Parks **[Fig. 1]**. Instead of postcard views, they reveal to each visitor a cross-section of the diverse conditions of the site. Both geological (*e.g.*, water, topography, forest cover) and extractive (*e.g.*, grazing, logging, mining) conditions are exposed alongside the access roads. The roads are bundled according to variations on the experience of a given site condition **[Fig. 3]**. For example, in a given bundle, one road may go through a mine site, another just outside the mine boundary, and yet another through a clearcut near the start of the road but avoid a later mine or range area. Perpendicular shunt roads connect the access roads at critical points, where tourists must make decisions according to their landscape preferences. In other words, as the unsuspecting tourist makes his way towards a campsite on a given access road and encounters site conditions contrary to his landscape values, he can take a shunt road and transfer to another path. In this way each tourist "votes with his feet" a crisis of public authority in which competing user groups challenge and demonize the National Forest Service. The National Forests are where understandings about the value of land clash most, where a variety of seemingly incompatible programs collide, and where very different user groups confront each other.

Negotiating the National Forests began as a prototype for dealing with the vast territory held by the National Forest Service. The project addresses and exploits the conditions in the National Forests through an architectural intervention within a 327,367-acre portion of Kaibab National Forest, just south of the Grand Canyon in northwestern Arizona. Kaibab's proximity to one of the nation's most famous National Parks allows for play between different notions of the meaning of public lands. The project focuses on an area between two transportation pathways: Highway 64, the only route providing access to and from the main portion of the Grand Canyon, and the Grand Canyon Railroad, a tourist line running into the park. Both of these routes pass through Kaibab, making the forest the threshold to the park.

Possession is Nine-Tenths of the Law

To show how architecture could play a role in land-use politics, the project began by examining existing infrastructure within Kaibab National Forest. Resource-extraction and ranching activities had a physical expression already—mining and logging roads, fences for cattle enclosures, water tanks and catchment basins, among other elements—whereas recreational and wilderness activities did not. Consequently, it followed that the project should involve the introduction of visitor-related infrastructure. This would give a physical presence to users without an economic stake in the forest, and import a wider range of environmental values, all in keeping with the constituent activities guaranteed by MUSY. Four million visitors a year travel through Kaibab on their way to the Grand Canyon National Park, but the Grand Canyon can only accommodate one million overnight stays per year. The remaining three million potential stays became the audience for this project and began to define the extents of the program.

Tourists in the Forests

This project embraces a series of contradictions: building a physical expression of environmental values without imposing any one discourse; playing legislated multiple use and physical multiple use against each other; and proposing infrastructure that increases tensions between users. It structures an uncertain outcome and sparks policy change rather than installing an infrastructure that reconciles users and remains static.

The fundamental operation of the project is to identify areas within Kaibab National Forest where the legislated boundaries of several user groups overlap and to insert visitors into those already-contested spaces. By intensifying physical proximity, the scheme forces users to confront the full repercussions of multiple use landscapes.

Tourists are drawn into the overlap zones as they seek out visitor services: campsites, visitor centers, hiking trails, restrooms, "event" areas, administrative buildings, ranger housing, and equipment storage. These comprise the typical amenities in the National Parks, altered here in placement and form to reflect the situation in the National Forests. To access these services, a series of parallel, straight roads penetrate the site, leading westward from Highway 64. These access roads contrast strongly with the picturesque routes typically designed in the National Parks [Fig. 1]. Instead of postcard views, they reveal to each visitor a cross-section of the diverse conditions of the site. Both geological (*e.g.*, water, topography, forest cover) and extractive (*e.g.*, grazing, logging, mining) conditions are exposed alongside the access roads. The roads are bundled according to variations on the experience of a given site condition [Fig. 3]. For example, in a given bundle, one road may go through a mine site, another just outside the mine boundary, and yet another through a clearcut near the start of the road but avoid a later mine or range area. Perpendicular shunt roads connect the access roads at critical points, where tourists must make decisions according to their landscape preferences. In other words, as the unsuspecting tourist makes his way towards a campsite on a given access road and encounters site conditions contrary to his landscape values, he can take a shunt road and transfer to another path. In this way each tourist "votes with his feet"

Figure 4

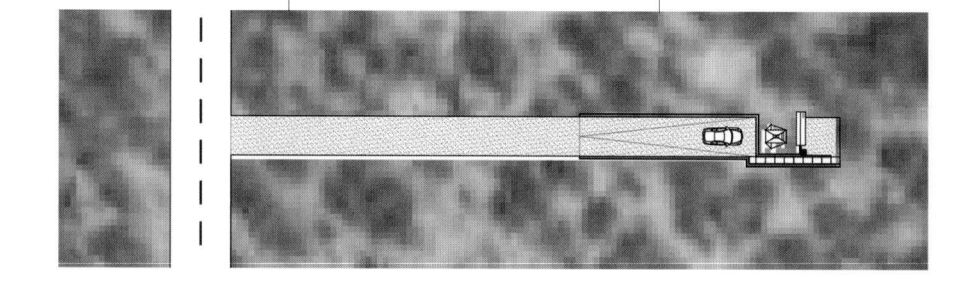

UPHILL

LEVEL

DOWNHILL

40 ft · 20 ft
30 ft · 10 ft

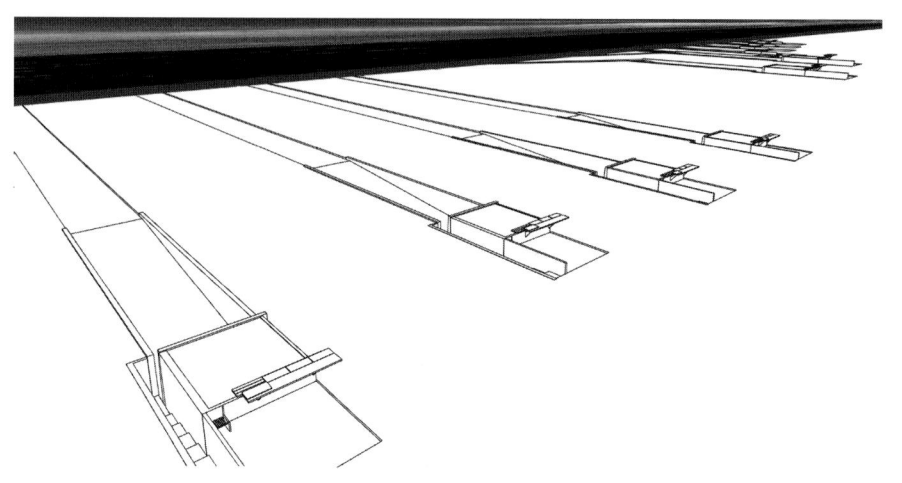

CAMPSITES

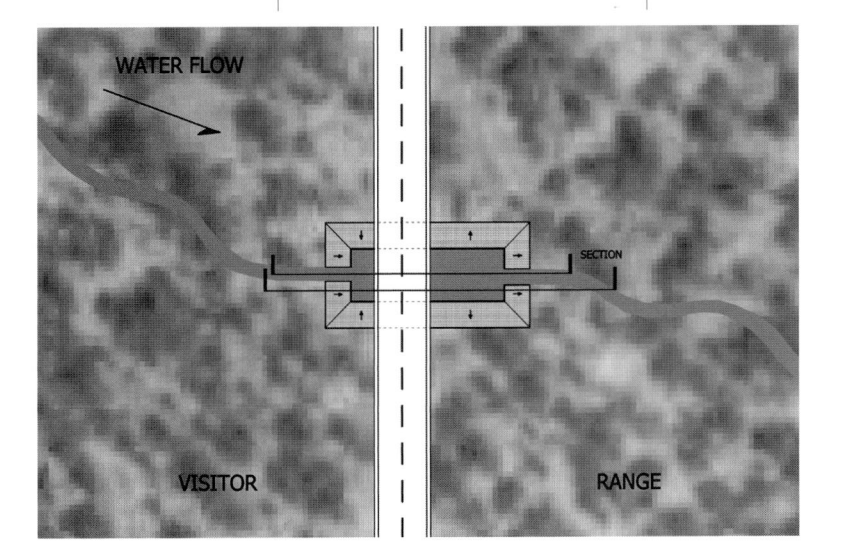

WATER FLOW

SECTION

VISITOR

RANGE

Figure 5

LOW WATER LEVELS
Water builds up at outer edge
of tank, until it builds up and
spills into tak.

WATER CHANNEL   GROUND LEVEL   ROAD

WATER FLOW

EQUILIBRIUM WATER LEVELS
Tank fills up to 4' line; if water continues to rise, water will flow out of
the tank on the other end.

HIGH WATER LEVELS
Tank is full; water will flow into and
through tank, continuing the water
course as if the tank weren't there.

40 ft   20 ft

30 ft   10 ft

STOCK TANKS

(or car), and the National Forest Service can track preferences based on the frequency with which each road and campsite is used.

Services are concentrated around clusters of parallel access roads and shunts. Service elements are tied into the various layers of the site **[Fig. 2]**, mitigating the orthogonal nature of the larger-scale elements. Campsites are situated along the parallel access roads but positioned according to topo lines. Though the same architectural element is used each time, a variety of conditions are produced with respect to the road and to other campsites. At night, burning campfires reveal the extent of the visitor system and show that the visitor—like other users on the site—is an active force within the landscape, not just a neutral observer. The architecture of the campsites plays on the visitor's relationship to his car, to other campers, and to views of the surrounding landscape **[Fig. 4]**. The campsites are built of a combination of permanent concrete elements and the (changing) surfaces of the landscape.

Visitor centers are located wherever the parallel access roads convert to trails. The centers consist of a series of mobile, reconfigurable pavilions placed along the forest edge, which is itself determined by clearcuts and regrowth and thereby changes over relatively short periods of time. Where the access and shunt roads meet the forest's intermittent waterways, stock tanks tie grazing and tourists together **[Fig. 5]**.

The Boundary Battle

The infrastructure described above is expected to change in unprescribed ways over time, depending on the site's ecology and the direction of land politics. Although certain hardscape elements will resist erasure, the infrastructure as a system is intended to be malleable and not necessarily durable.

As various parties react to the newly-installed visitor infrastructure, they will almost certainly seek political change in the form of redrawn boundaries. For example, ranchers and loggers may request that lawmakers move their parcels away from tourists for reasons of convenience and public relations. However, new boundaries inevitably mean new overlaps, which in turn mean more sites for

visitor services. This sustained visitor presence will either hound other users until the amenities for three million overnight stays is reached, or until conflict between user groups forces a final set of priorities in National Forest legislation **[Fig. 6]**.

Those priorities could be resolved in a number of ways. A single user group could be granted exclusive rights, leading to the dismantling of alternative infrastructures. A group of extractive users could be given explicit priority over visitors, halting the existence of overlaps and hence the expansion of visitor programs. Or, perhaps most unfortunately, the conflict could continue indefinitely, causing visitor infrastructure to sprawl over much of the site, diminishing its attraction for tourists and leading to its abandonment altogether.

Conclusions

Although admittedly cynical, *Negotiating the National Forests* suggests how architecture might influence land politics and help organize the way the American public understands its relationship to landscape. In this way, architecture can help the public come to a decision about how and why it values landscape—not by suppressing the plurality of divergent opinions, but by revealing and juxtaposing them so that they can be compared and critiqued.

Claire H. Johnson, *M.Arch. (Princeton, 2003), is an architect currently living and working in New York City. Her work focuses on environmental thought in architectural theory and design. Her thesis,* Negotiating the National Forests, *was carried out at Princeton under the guidance of Stan Allen.*

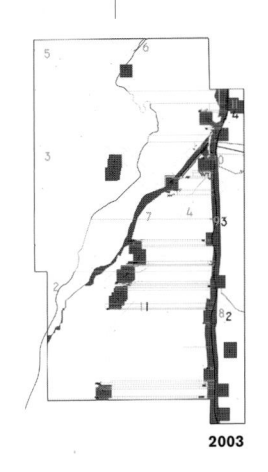

2003

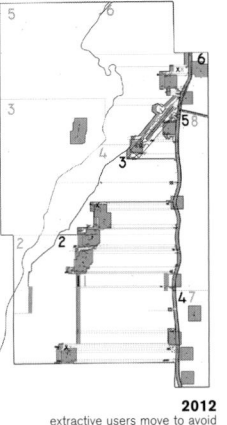
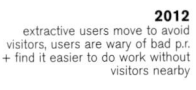

2012
extractive users move to avoid
visitors, users are wary of bad p.r.
+ find it easier to do work without
visitors nearby

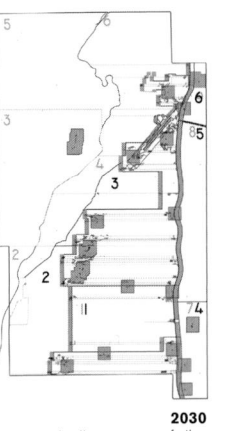

2030
extractive users move farther

2045
user backlash: extractive users
move back into visitor areas, where
resources have been regenerating
for ~50 years

2060
resolution #1: visitors have priorities, followed by loggers, ranchers,
and miners

**2060:
three potential resolutions**

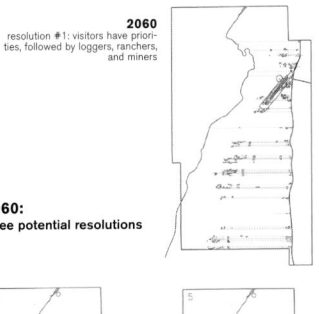
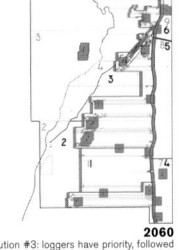
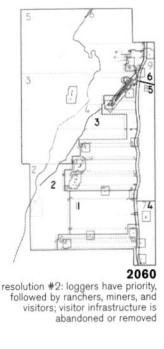

2060
resolution #3: loggers have priority, followed
by visitors, miners, and ranchers; visitor infrastructure near highway is used; other installations are abandoned or removed

2060
resolution #2: loggers have priority,
followed by ranchers, miners, and
visitors; visitor infrastructure is
abandoned or removed

Figure 6

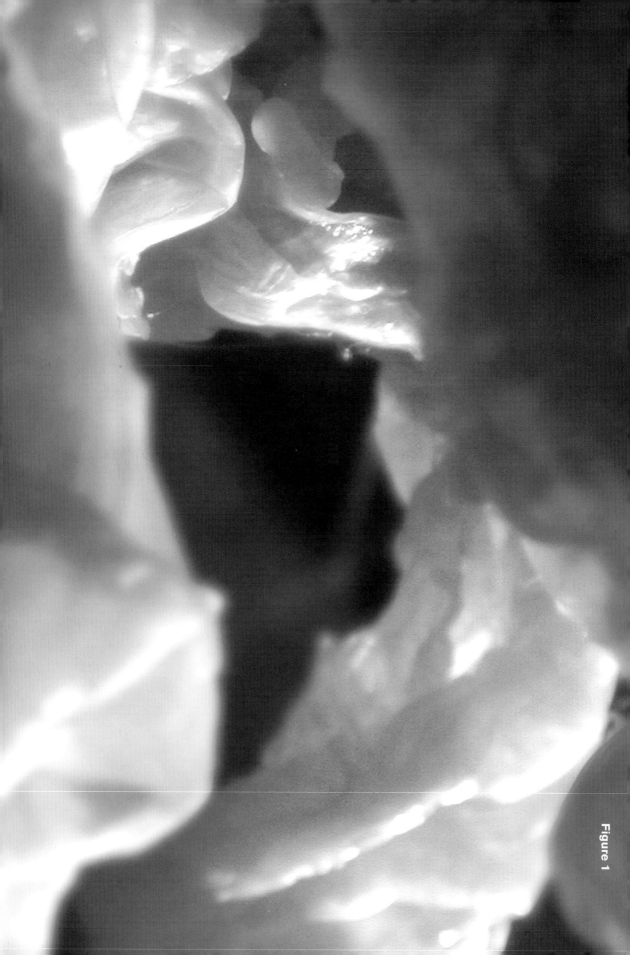

Figure 1

MEMORY AND METAMORPHOSIS

CONNECTION THROUGH IMMERSION

Elena Wiersma

How do we access the wild?

How deeply am I willing to go into the wilderness?

This Master of Architecture thesis asks these questions by using created and imagined cathartic experiences to access the wilderness of the land, our bodies, and our minds. The threshold between the inner wilderness, or our unconscious, and the outer wilderness, or the natural world, is explored through installations, models, collages, writing, and personal journal entries (shown here in italics). The second growth remnant of wilderness chosen for the thesis site is located on the Bruce Peninsula within Bruce Peninsula National Park, Ontario, Canada. The thesis is a critical response to Bruce Peninsula National Park's plan to build a new visitor center on a very tame site far from the wild shores of Georgian Bay. **[Fig. 2]** The images and text that follow portray an architectural fantasy that proposes, instead, to inhabit the interior landscape of the Bruce Peninsula.

Here, the wilderness is found under the clear waters of Georgian Bay, in the adjacent cedar forest, and inside the rock of the Bruce Peninsula itself. A careful study of photographs taken while visiting the site led to extensive research concerning the geological origin and karst landscape of the rock. Images of the site's surfaces, which

Figure 2

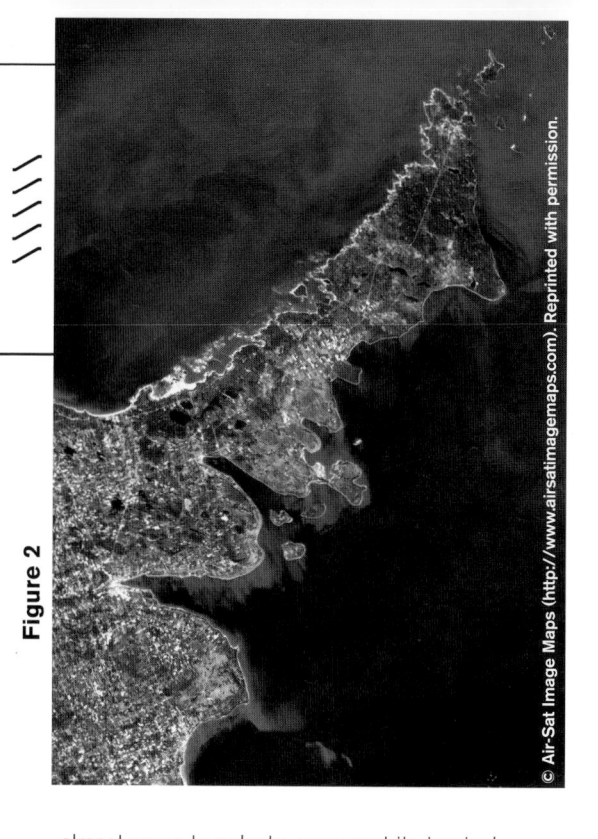

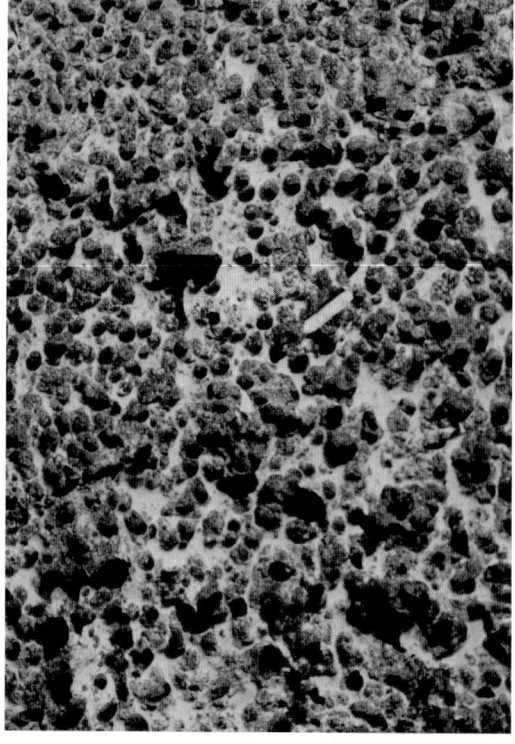

Figure 3

almost seem to pulsate, represent its tropical, watery origin and its metamorphosis into the present wild landscape. **[Figs. 3-6]**

Models were used to speculate on the forms carved by the labyrinth of water contained within the rock of the Bruce Peninsula. Sectional cuts through a plaster model reveal inhabitable spaces and intricate patterns carved by water. **[Figs. 7 & 8]** Acrylic contour models facilitate a sense of immersion into the interior of the ancient lime-stone and dolostone bedrock. The first model displays imagined caverns carved by water within the rock and represents possible routes of human passage through the rock. **[Figs. 9]** The second model represents a section of the Bruce Peninsula extending into Georgian Bay and is a tool to help viewers grasp the complexity of the porous bedrock. **[Figs. 10 & 11]**

In the proposed scheme, an access and guid-ance system enables people to climb down into fissures and caverns, mimicking cedar tree roots on the site. Flexible stainless steel attachments and fittings are inserted into fissures in the rock and hold a network of cedar roots imported to the site from harvested forests. The stainless steel structure mimics fossils, or coral bones, and the roots age and become part of the landscape. **[Fig. 12]**

I come to a large fissure in the rock. As I look more closely, the fissure has an access system of cedar roots raised off the rock. I climb down the roots into the dark, cool cavern. The root system is flexible and adjusts by rotating slightly when I put my weight on it.

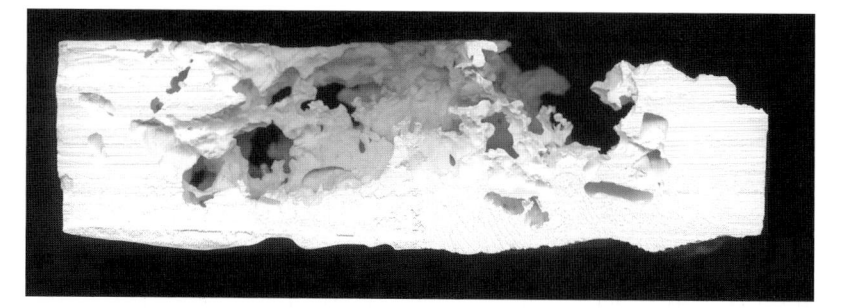

Figure 4

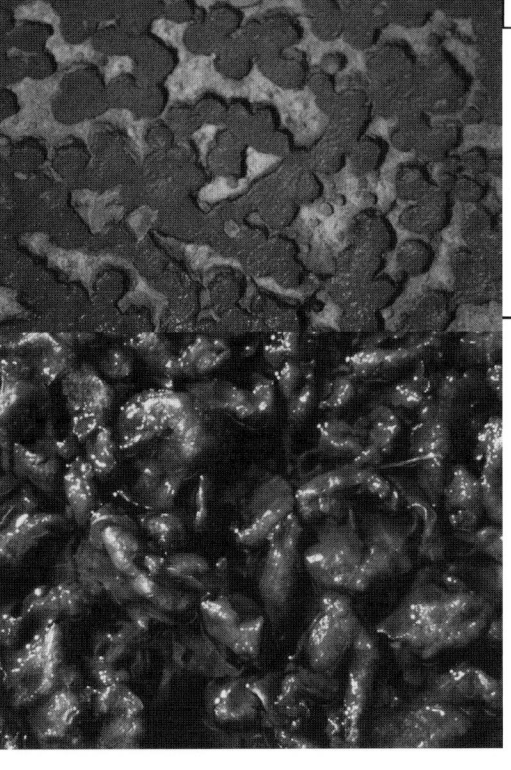

Figures 5 & 6

A cross sectional collage through the porous bedrock of the Bruce Peninsula, based on geological research and visits to the site, portrays an internal landscape carved by water and inhabitable by humans. The section extends from the top of the cliff plateau to the bottom of Georgian Bay. **[Figs. 13 & 14]**

The cave is dark except for the shafts of light shining down through fissures in the rock, exposing patterns and fossils. I hear the sound of the water filtering through the rock. In places the cavern is very small. The contours of my body must adjust to the contours of the unforgiving passageways. The rock is cold and when I touch it I feel the heat leaving my body.

A latex model presents the unconscious or negative of the Bruce Peninsula by depicting the caverns as a hovering network of intestines below the surface of the earth. The model represents the dark spaces of the caverns and the wilderness of our unconscious. **[Fig. 1]**

I navigate through the caverns following the flow of the water and moving between light shafts. Penetrating the rock is like penetrating my unconscious; it is intimidating but rewarding. I long for the rock to open up to a larger space, for a release. Finally I emerge from the cave into the light and the summer heat. I am standing on the shore of and immense turquoise bay.

The geology of the Bruce Peninsula tells a

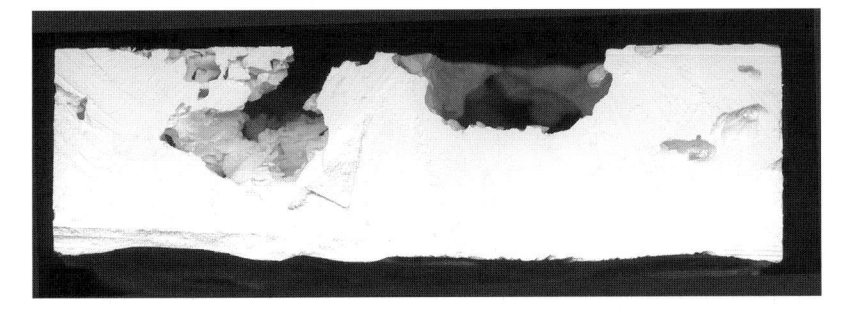

Figures 8

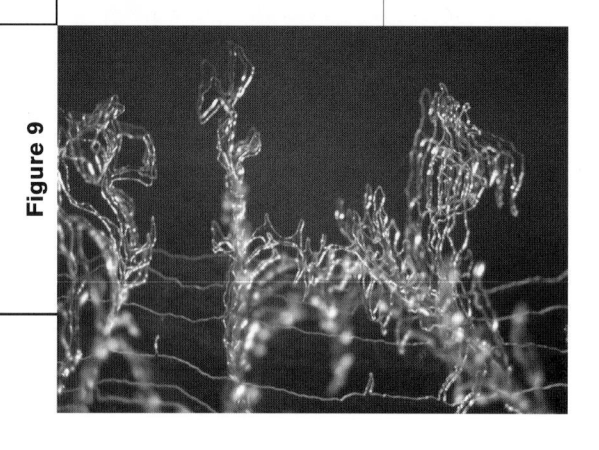

Figure 9

story of transformation from liquid seas to solid rock. The investigations of this thesis transform our understanding of the site from solid rock to porous labyrinth. In contrast to the park's philosophy of interpreting the wilderness through a building set apart from the wild, the schematic and imagined access proposal of the thesis do not control or tame the wilderness. The wild space of the interior of the rock of the Bruce Peninsula crosses the boundary of personal safety and loss of identity, and revels in the unconscious. It is through our own inner wild that we respond to the natural and relate to the remaining wilderness.

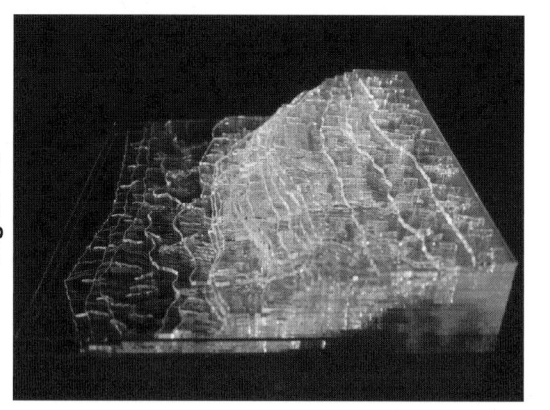

Figure 10

Figure 11

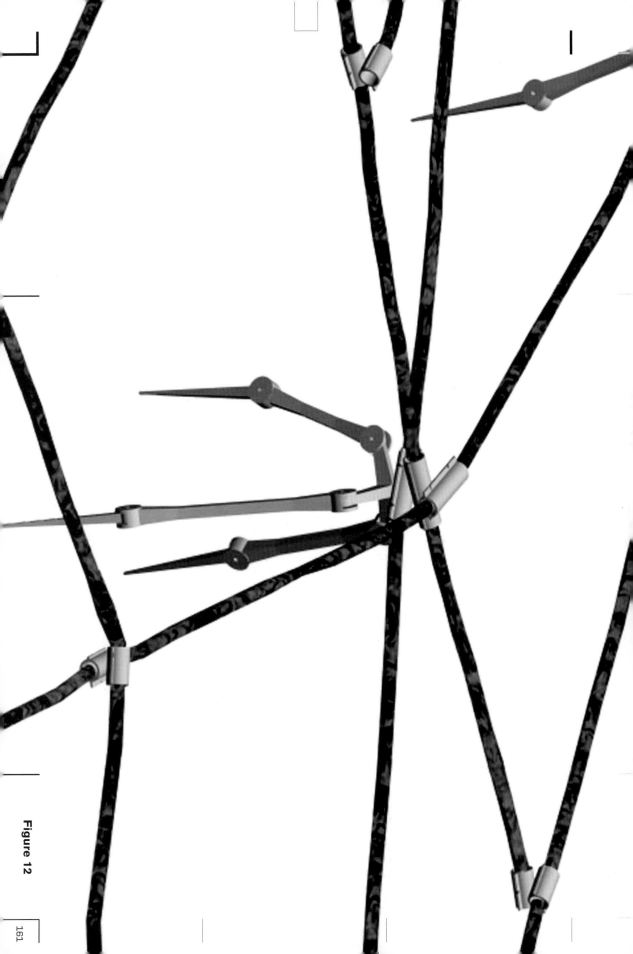

Figure 12

161

Figures 13 & 14

Elena Wiersma, *M.Arch. (University of Waterloo, 2002), currently lives and works in Kitchener, Ontario. Her thesis, Memory and Metamorphosis: Connection Through Immersion, was awarded the 2003 Royal Architectural Institute of Canada Student Medal for the University of Waterloo.*

48 mo.

Figure 1

Figure 2

Figure 3

SEA CHANGE or, IMPENDING DUNE

Kristin Schuster

The slow disaster of shoreline erosion has been met with various attempts to control the relationship between Galveston Island and the Gulf of Mexico. In territorializing the island as private property, the main economic draw (the beach) is being sacrificed as the sandbar is increasingly expected to behave like a stable landmass. Private Property Rights and Public Beach Access clash as the difference between the land and the sea refuses to manifest itself as a line drawn through space.

There is latent potential within the instability of the land itself to work with a beach access infrastructure that operates as a mesh. Such a system can transgress problematic territorial boundaries and mark out multiple processes of reterritorialization as they are occurring on the site. In this way, the forces at work in shaping the island can become culturally relevant in a constructive way, altering the human relationship with the land.

Siting the Disaster

As a heavily developed coastal barrier island, Galveston is plagued by disasters. There is the sudden disaster—the intermittent bombardment of the island by tropical storms and hurricanes—and there is the slow disaster—the alarming rate at which the island's beaches are eroding. Shoreline erosion and storm damage are treated as separate disasters, even though their effects are linked: the beaches and dunes are the island's natural defenses against storm effects.

Once the economic capital of the Texas Gulf Coast, the City of Galveston is now a struggling tourist town. Potential in the form of property tax revenue from as yet undeveloped land and increased visitor traffic are bringing local government to push for development of nearly all of the remaining open land on the island in the form of second home development on the island's West End.[1] Although this means increased revenue for the city and county, the foundation of this economy is federal money in the form of subsidized insurance and disaster mitigation funds.[2] These subsidies support high values for the private property that is threatened by the natural events that shape the land. In response, erosion and storms are met with resistive counter-measures that protect private property on the island at the further financial expense of county and federal taxpayers as well as the physical expense of the coastal environment.

Traditional protective measures such as the eleven-mile-long Galveston Seawall have been deemed too costly to continue to build and maintain.[3] Geotextile tubes are the latest technology employed to battle flooding and the creeping property line. Intended to replace eroded dunes and protect the hinterland by not allowing the shoreline to move landward, these resistive measures redirect the forces further down the island, causing increased erosion and beach loss in front of other unprotected property. While Geotubes are often billed as beach protection, they function as private property protection. Because sand continues to wash away while the stabilized shoreline ceases to move back, the beach disappears completely in front of these structures. As wave energy is not absorbed the unprotected property adjacent to them will erode at an increased rate. **[Fig. 4]**

As a result of this process, the Texas General Land Office has designated West Galveston Island, the twenty-one miles of island down-stream of the seawall, a critical erosion area. Due to the channelization of the Mississippi River, which diverted up-stream sand sources, and the development of the Houston Ship channel, sand migration on Galveston Island functions at a deficit of 700,000 cubic yards each year.[4] At the Western end of

the seawall, the beach erosion rate is in excess of fifteen feet per year.[5]

To counter this, beaches are currently rebuilt along Galveston's shore through a process called beach nourishment, which involves replacing the sand that migrates off of Galveston beaches each year. Not a permanent solution, beach nourishment must be repeated periodically as sand continues to be lost. This process relies on the availability of compatible sand supplies, which are increasingly rare.

It is notable that the property that is disappearing sells for $850 per linear foot of beachfront, and generates $34,000,000 in property tax revenue each year.[6] This explains why of the

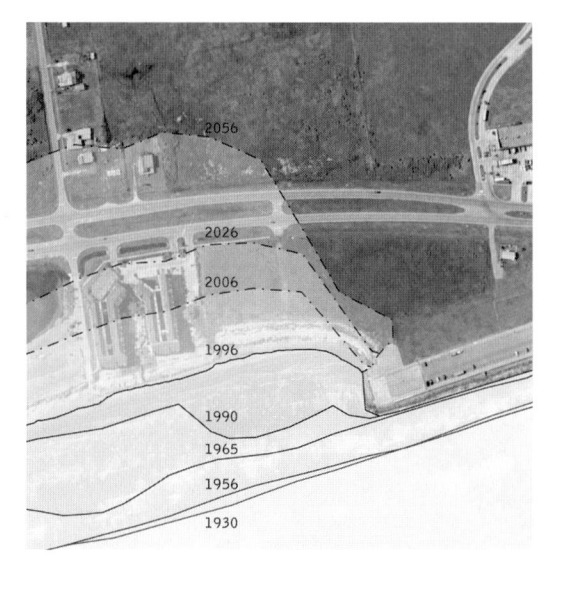

twelve factors considered in the determination of a critical erosion area designation, private and personal loss is considered the most important while public access is third, public safety is eleventh, and human activity ranks as the least important factor taken into consideration.[7] Ironically, the beaches that are sacrificed by property protection strategies are the foundation of the tourism economy.

That private losses currently rank more critically than public access, safety, and human activity is particularly significant considering the historical and political relationship between Texans and their beaches. Texas is unusual in that beaches are public (state) property. In 1977 the Texas Open Beaches Act (TOBA) legally established that "the area extending from the line of mean low tide of the Gulf of Mexico to the line of vegetation bordering on the Gulf of Mexico" is public beach.[8] The main focus of the TOBA is to ensure unrestricted access by the public to any publicly owned beach, primarily by disallowing construction that blocks beach access. While it seems completely unexceptional that private construction not be allowed on public land, the unstable nature of the shoreline in conjunction with the particular legal definition of the public property boundary set up by the TOBA creates a condition of perpetual conflict and struggle between private property rights and public access. In short, the property line is always moving. Buildings that cross the boundary

Drawing the Line

This perception is based on traditional models of barrier island formation, which conceptualize the island on a macroscopic scale as a cohesive mass of drifting sand—a kind of solid, if mobile, landmass.[9] The trouble with these timeless abstractions is that they allow us to consider the island in a way that causes our structures to be physically incompatible with the landscape. This incompatibility becomes most obvious at moments of disastrous structural failure as houses collapse into the sea after sand is eroded around their foundations. It can also be seen in the struggle for beach maintenance by property rights groups, as technologies based on these models are even further incapable of addressing the ambiguity between public and private. The tools and technologies currently used to design and construct in these environments treat them as fixed topography, as does the legal

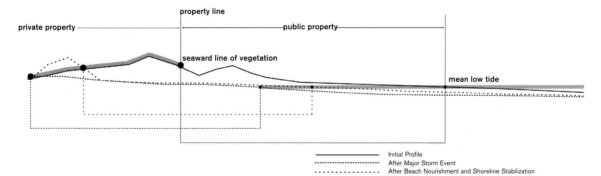

property line

private property —————————— ————public property————

seaward line of vegetation

mean low tide

——————— Initial Profile
························· After Major Storm Event
– – – – – – – After Beach Nourishment and Shoreline Stabilization

and become partially or fully on public land due to processes of erosion must be removed. From the perspective of the private property owner, the natural formal cycle of the island is a disaster. **[Fig. 5]**

The disaster that plagues Galveston Island is the collision between private property rights and public access to public land. The disaster is the economic collision between the forces that have shaped the island and Gulf Coast over thousands of years, and the people who don't recognize them and thus claim ownership of the land. The disaster is not that the shoreline moves—the disaster is the fact that it is expected not to. The disaster is the perception of the land.

definition of the land. The primary assertion of the Texas Open Beaches Act establishes a line that is not a line at all. A new concept of the island is required, one based on an understanding of the island as an environment of forces. Such a conception requires new ways of building on the island and understanding what it means to do so. This understanding could lead to economically sustainable tourism-based modes of human activity and presence that directly confront notions of private property rights as currently practiced on Galveston Island. The first step is to engage the processes, and rectify the social relationship with them.

Modeling the Site

This project defines the island as a slurry—a semi-liquid mixture of sand and water in different ratios—rather than as a drifting mass of sand. There is no delineable distinction between the island and the body of water surrounding it, nor between the public beach and the private hinterland. The lines of mean low tide and vegetation are ill-conceived as lines. This understanding of the island site gives credibility to the tidal, wave, wind, current, and submergence forces that have been identified as active in island formation by recognizing that they are perpetually active. They are not separate from nor located outside the island, but rather material conditions of difference within it.

The tools and technologies exist to work within this concept. Whereas a topographic map renders the site as solid, passive, and receptive, a vector drawing models a slurry that is alive with actively willful behaviors. By drawing the site as flow and form rather than topographic configuration, vector drawing allows the design to be based on the relationships present within the site which remain constant even as the configuration changes. In dealing with an unfixed site, designing for the relationships rather than the configuration ensures the relevance of the intervention beyond the dissolution of the current configuration.

Figures 6-9 reveal the complex relationship between the weather and the landscape as they are traditionally conceptualized. Each is an iteration built on the previous, a rendering of the forces and forms present at the site over one calendar year. More importantly, these drawings provide formal and operational implications for the proposed system of beach access, as well as the foundation for a three-dimensional CAD drawing process to test and represent the final design proposal for beach access.

To recognize that the landscape is active gives new imperative to the act of intervening. To intervene in such a site is to harness the activity of the site, redirecting the energy of the slurry to effect the desired change indirectly. The landscape will do the work. The intervention must remain viable in the kinetic environment, and it must be flexible enough to ride with the slurry. In other words, it will function at the level of the relationships within the slurry, and the relationship between the slurry and humans.

Meshes are the ideal structures in such an environment, having both structure and flexibility. A mesh with inherent structural properties, such as a pleated textile, will support the functional interests of human activity while strategically mediating the behavior of the slurry. The flexibility of such a mesh is limited by the size of the pleats and their orientation in relationship to overall size of the

Figures 6-9

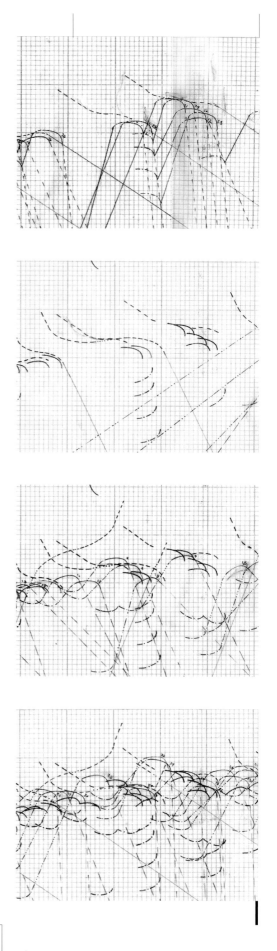

piece of material. Thus, for the scale of application relative to the scale of the pleats necessary to give the given material structure, a panel size can be determined. The use of a panel system allows for added flexibility in the deformations, while strategically controlling connections between panels and layering of different material types can add greater sensitivity to specific conditions of the slurry.

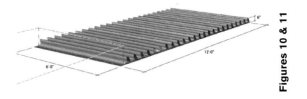

Blurring the Line

The proposed beach access infrastructure takes the form of a system of geotextile panels in order to take advantage of the natural abilities of a mesh to strategically mediate the behavior of both people and a slurry. **[Figs. 10 & 11]** There are three panel types, each of which corresponds to different conditions within the slurry. Each panel corresponds to a zone of the site, and is able to mediate both the slurry and human circulation in the specific ways noted due to construction of the layered section and combination of the materials used. Each panel is anchored in the slurry at only two points, the center of the short edges. As a result, the panel is able to radically deform to accommodate the current configuration of the landscape and the total panel construction in order to remain viable as a system of beach access that is traversable by humans. The combination of unidirectional pleats, spring straps, and a dimensionally stable edge ribbon create specific deformational behaviors that both impact the smoothness of the resulting configuration and add significant sectional characteristics which mediate and channel circulation at another scale. **[Fig. 12]** As paths are no longer traversable, new panels must be connected to the system. The result is a constantly configuring system of pathways that operate according to the physical principles of the ecology rather than the territorial logic of human occupation.

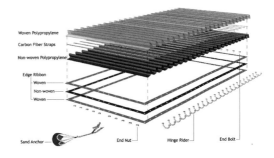

The pathways literally blur and stretch the legal boundaries of the site. Physically, the system allows the forces present to produce dry beach and dunes as sand is scooped up and channeled inland. **[Figs. 13-17]** Without the system installed, the beach will not exist, having been sacrificed in futile attempts to halt the erasure of the private property inland of it. Without the beach, the island's $350,000,000 tourism economy would suffer. Politically, the system inverts the current set of priorities which value private property rights over public access to the beach. Due to the physical effects of the intervention, beach access would become a desirable element on private property, whereas now it is often illegally removed or obscured by private property owners wishing to exclude the public from their land and vistas.

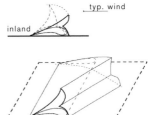

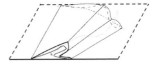

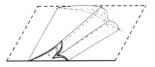

Figure 12

Fundamentally, the system makes the workings of the forces within the landscape visible and serves as a marker for the work they can do. Erosion transforms into a productive process as island change becomes real in the popular concept of the place. **[Figs. 1-3]** By upending the popular conception of the coastal landscape, this project lays a path for dialogue about building technologies and land-use policies more appropriate in a fluid landscape.

Kristin Schuster, *M.Arch. (Rice University, 2003), is currently living and working in San Francisco. Her master's thesis,* Sea Change, or impending dune, *was completed under the direction of Nana Last, with special thanks to David Brown, Albert Pope, Dawn Finley and Luke Bulman.*

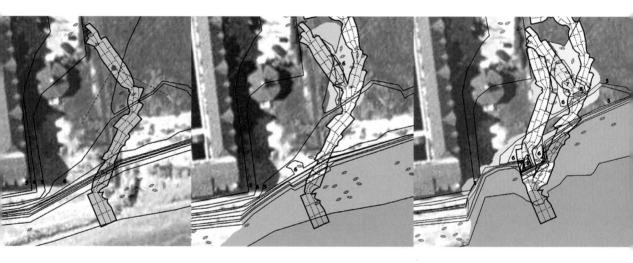

NOTES

1 _ See http://recenter.tamu.edu/ mreports/GalvestonTCity2.asp (Real Estate Center of the Mays Business School, Texas A&M University).
2 _ Homeowners on Galveston are required to carry Windstorm, Flood, and Hazard Insurance. These policies are not supportable on the insurance market, so the government steps in with the Federal Insurance Management Agency, Texas Windstorm Insurance Association, and the Texas Catastrophe Property Insurance Pool to provide the

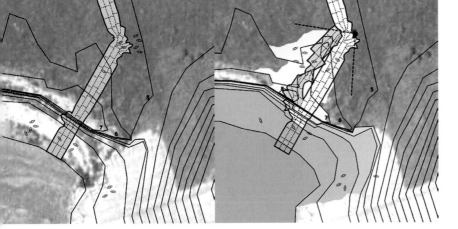

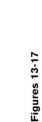

required coverage and affordable rates.
3 _ More information on coastal engineering can be found online through the United States Army Corps of Engineers at http://www.swg.usace.army.mil/
4 _ This information comes from a 13 September 2002 telephone interview with Thomas Ravens of the Department of Maritime Systems Engineering at Texas A&M University, Galveston.
5 _ For in-depth information about shoreline change on the Texas Gulf Coast, see the Texas Shoreline Change Project of the Bureau of Economic Geology, Coastal Studies Group website http://www.beg.utexas.

edu/coastal/intro.htm) or that of the Rice University Coastal Research Group (http://gulf.rice.edu/coastal)
6 _ This information was gained from Galveston County and Galveston City Annual Budgets for the years 1993, 1995, and 1998.
7 _ Texas General Land Office Advisory Board, 12 July 1995.
8 _ Chapter 61 of the Texas Natural Resources Code, also known as the Texas Open Beaches Act, can be found in its entirety on the website of the Texas General Land office at http://www.glo.state.tx.us/
9 _ For an in-depth explanation of the Hoyt Beach Ridge Submergence

Theory of Barrier Island Formation, see http://www.salem.mass.edu/~lhanson/gls214_barrier_isl.htm

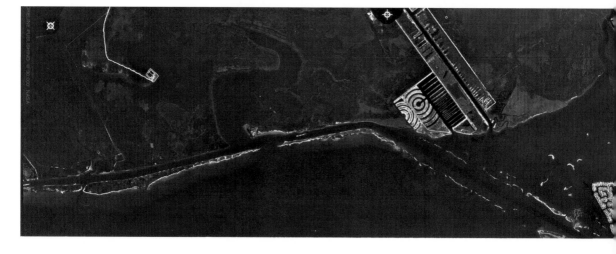

FLAMINGO ISLE

Chula Ross Sanchez

The 3,600 acre site on the Intracoastal Waterway was dredged beginning circa 1961. Houston oilman, John Mecom, had a vision of a city for 100,000+ residents, a *Xanadu* by the sea, carved from primordial wetlands. The project was abandoned in 1967.

A proposal of minimal intervention.
Access exclusively by water.
A floating dock for disembarkation, transition.
The footpath, meandering along the edges of
      the manmade geometry,
         through the ruins, rest and shade every half mile.
Glass markers, Moonbeams, *where path and cosmic compass align,*
         growing as the land recedes,
         recording time and place.
The Lighthouse, the destination point, one of prospect.
An observation platform rising above the ruins.
         A gift of sweeping vistas over the land,
         down the coast and into the sky.
An opportunity for reconciliation.

Beside Flamingo Isle

Forbidden territory, ruins in wait,
natural beauty–mystery.
A dinner party table
set forty years ago, the guests,
now long gone; champagne still
in some of the cups. So what will you do?
Clean up the party, wash the linens,
sweep out the cobwebs and move in?
Or just brush away the crumbs
so as not to attract the varmints
and leave the rest as memory, like a footprint?
Or do you, grateful, just walk away?

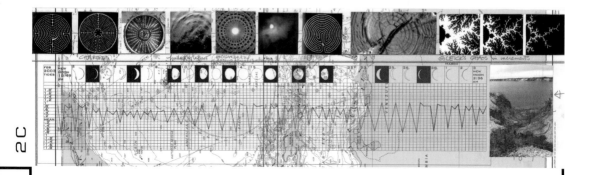

Unsurveyed

Moving Forward

*The deep parts of my life pour onward,
as if the river shores were opening out.
It seems that things are more like me now,
that I can see farther into paintings.
I feel closer to what language can't reach.
With my senses, as with birds, I climb
into the windy heaven, out of the oak,
and in the ponds broken off from the sky
my feeling sinks, as if standing on fishes.*

///// Ranier Maria Rilke

"A monument [...] is venerated not as a work of art or as an antique, but as an echo from the remote past suddenly become present and actual."

///// J.B. Jackson, *The Necessity for Ruins* (Amherst: University of Massachusetts Press, 1980), 91.

"*Still all the while, like warp and woof, mechanism and teleology are interwoven together and we must not cleave to the one nor despise the other; for their very union is rooted in the very nature of totality.*"

///// D'Arcy Wentworth Thompson, *On Growth and Form* (New York: Dover Publications, 1992; first published by Cambridge University Press, 1942), 7.

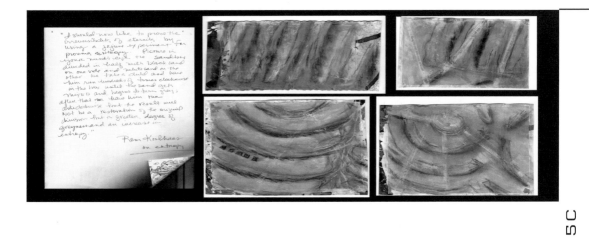

100 years from now,
left alone, Flamingo Isle will return to
the tidal flats, reconfigured from its origins.
The edges melting with the intermittent
                cycles of the tides, wind, water,
                        and man's participation on the edge.

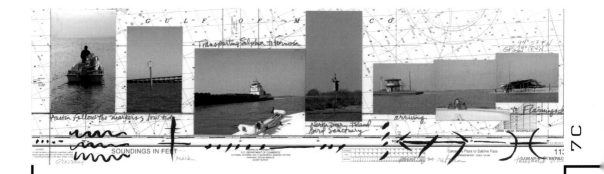

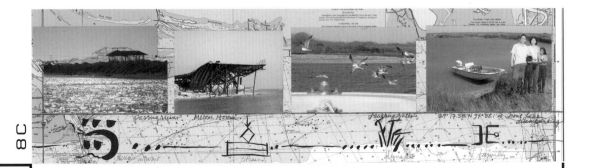

I'm afraid of it, but always make an excuse to go back, another photo, something I haven't seen. It's push & pull—a Chinese finger puzzle.

Ronnie sent this to me in an email:
in *Art Matters*, Peter de Bolla described wonderment this way:
"Wonder requires us to acknowledge what we do not know or may never know, to acknowledge the limits of knowledge. It is, then a different species of knowledge, a way of knowing that does not lead to certainties or truths about the world or the way things are. It is a state of mind that, like being in love, colors all that we know."

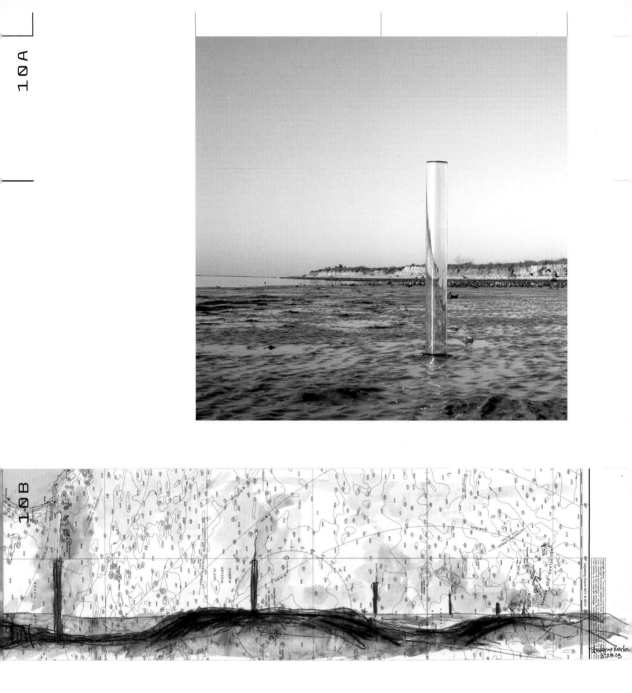

EPILOGUE:

1. **Planning is a process.   TIME**.

Layers of information (natural resources, cultural, spiritual, economic, etc.) reveal patterns helping to guide the process. The end is not the goal, but another stop along the way. There are no formulas, only a myriad of choices. Anticipation, phases, and flexibility provide for human participation and interpretation over time and space.

2. **Reconciliation.   PLACE**

Make peace with the dynamic equilibrium of opposites: cartesian and organic, the labyrinth and the grid, structure and chaos, nature and man, knowledge and myth, with man as the gatekeeper, as Jung put it, the ego, sitting at the threshold between the conscious world and the unconscious. Architecture is built by man, therefore, the physical intervention and interpretation are what give this project meaning.

3. **The Big Picture.   MEMORY**

The aerial view: the hawk's keen eye lets him see patterns in the landscape (structure); it's the quick darting of the mouse (deviation) that he discerns, and then goes in for the kill. In the urban setting, Roland Barthes' view from the Eiffel Tower is similar in that the viewer structures, categorizes, separates and then links; he called it decipherment. A system for memory making.

Flamingo Isle was recently purchased by a development corporation and is in the master planning stage for waterfront residences. A bridge over the Highland Bayou Diversionary Canal was completed in June 2003, allowing access by car from I-45.

Chula Ross Sanchez, M.Arch. (University of Houston, 2003), is an architect now living on Galveston Island and working in the Galveston/Houston area. Her project, Flamingo Isle, received the University of Houston's Gerald D. Hines College of Architecture Graduation Honor Design Award, with Special Commendation by the jury.

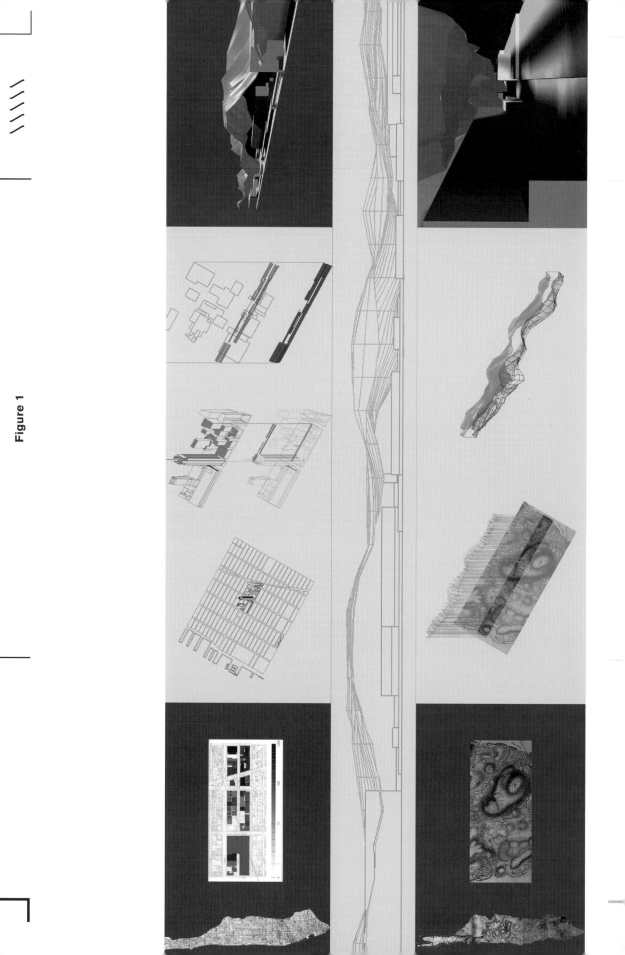

Figure 1

THE FIGURAL TIME OF LANDSCAPE

Penley Chiang

"The invisible forces, the powers of the future —are they not already upon us, and much more insurmountable than the worst spectacle and even the worst pain? Yes, in a certain sense— every piece of meat testifies to this. But in another sense, no. When, like a wrestler, the visible body confronts the powers of the invisible, it gives them no other visibility than its own. It is in this visibility that the body actively struggles, affirming the possibility of triumphing, which was beyond its reach as long as these powers remained invisible, hidden in a spectacle that sapped our strength and diverted us. It is as if combat had now become possible. The struggle with the shadow is the only real struggle.*"* [1]

///// Gilles Deleuze

I.

This project was carried out both as a graduate thesis at the University of Virginia and as part of a seminar there about what were dubbed (un)common spaces: spaces that are both common because of their ubiquity in our environ-ments today yet uncommon because of their resistance to meaningful inhabitation.[2] Such spaces are as diverse as parking lots, strip malls, landfills, overpasses, brownfields, airports,

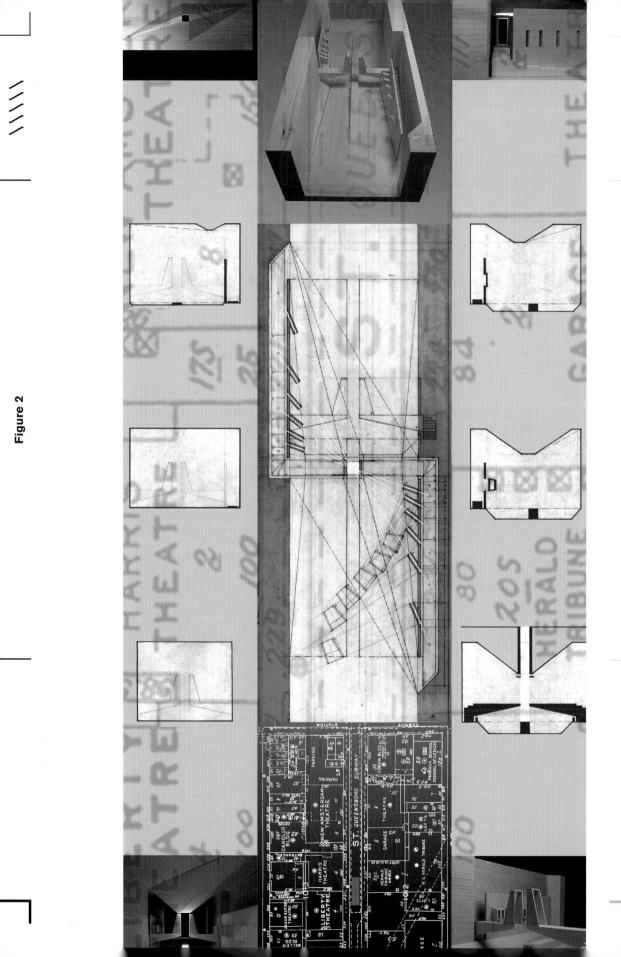

Figure 2

railyards, Superfund sites, highway medians, and—of course—those infrastructures or zones that are neither quite architecture nor landscape. Landscape *within* architecture, however, implies a more precise relationship between the two that is not so much a blurring or hybridity, but rather a colonization or invasion by one discipline from the interior of another: while the image and praxis of architecture may remain, its values have been hollowed out and overtaken by those of landscape.

II.

In the film *The Matrix*,[3] the protagonist Neo discovers that the world as he knows it is actually a computer-generated hallucination designed to keep humanity enslaved. By the end of the film, exhorted by his mentor and comrade Morpheus to "free your mind," Neo attains the ability to see past the illusory world of figural representation to perceive the streaming fields of code that condition its "reality". Architecturally speaking, the allegory is obvious enough. Because of globalization, media, information technology, terrorism, etc., architecture today finds itself in a besieged position, with not an inconsiderable amount of guilt and resentment with respect to its *being*: i.e., material, sessile, discrete, and relatively enduring. The dumb, object reality of architecture, so the thinking goes, must be sublimated on a virtual level capable of organizing flows, affects, events, becomings, etc.—everything that architecture itself is not. Thus, landscape—characterized by continuity, complexity, and connectivity—seems ideally poised to serve a paradigmatic function for architecture. As Winy Maas has noted, "Landscape is in the air! Landscape is everywhere! The word 'landscape' has so much zipped into the recent architectural discourse, that it is even more often used than Americans use the word 'fuck'."[4]

Yet, as another scene in *The Matrix* suggests, it may be premature to simply proclaim *death to the object!* and *long live the field!* The traitor Cypher, viewing several screens of fluctuating code, tells Neo that "there's way too much information to decode the matrix. You get used to it. I don't even see the code; all I see is blonde... brunette... redhead." Superficially, this betrayal of the field in favor of the figure seems to be a regres-

sion from Neo's achievement. However, is this not a truer description of how landscape within architecture can effectively (and affectively) operate *at the level of the subject*? From the overwhelming multiplicity of variables that constitute the field, Cypher's hacker intuition can apperceive the emergent molar effects of the molecular interactions of the matrix. That is, a provisional return of the figure may very well serve as a relay or point of access through which we, as (molar, conscious) subjects, can perceive, manipulate, or otherwise relate to the normally subterranean matrix of determinants that condition our environments. In this sense, the architectural figure becomes a fulcrum or focusing element without which the landscape (of systems, events, or information) would once again recede below the threshold of our immediate awareness. There is, of course, nothing mandating that the figure be a formal construct or even a material one; it is now just as likely to be an experience as something that can be represented graphically. This is because the corollaries to (un)common spaces are (un)common *times*. These are the durations we encounter as the supplement of other activities; they include time spent riding in the subway or on the escalator, stuck in traffic, in a layover at an airport, or waiting for a web page to load.

According to Heidegger, building produces dwelling into presence, meaning that in order truly to build, one must first know how to dwell—i.e., to cultivate a holistic relation with the world.[5] In a close reading of Heidegger, Massimo Cacciari concurs that it is precisely this spirit of dwelling to which we no longer have access.[6] Rather than a residing and a preserving, the dominant conditions today are transience and uprootedness, as demonstrated by the saturation of (un)common time:

"Non-dwelling is the essential characteristic of life in the metropolis [...] The 'history' of contemporary architecture is therefore a phenomenology of metropolitan non-dwelling. Or should be as such, since contemporary architecture aims at restructuring itself as the possibility of dwelling within the metropolis."[7]

Thus, against all efforts to reinscribe a (false) locus of dwelling within contemporary life, Cacciari argues that the task of architecture is to speak precisely of the absence of dwelling; it must

Figure 3

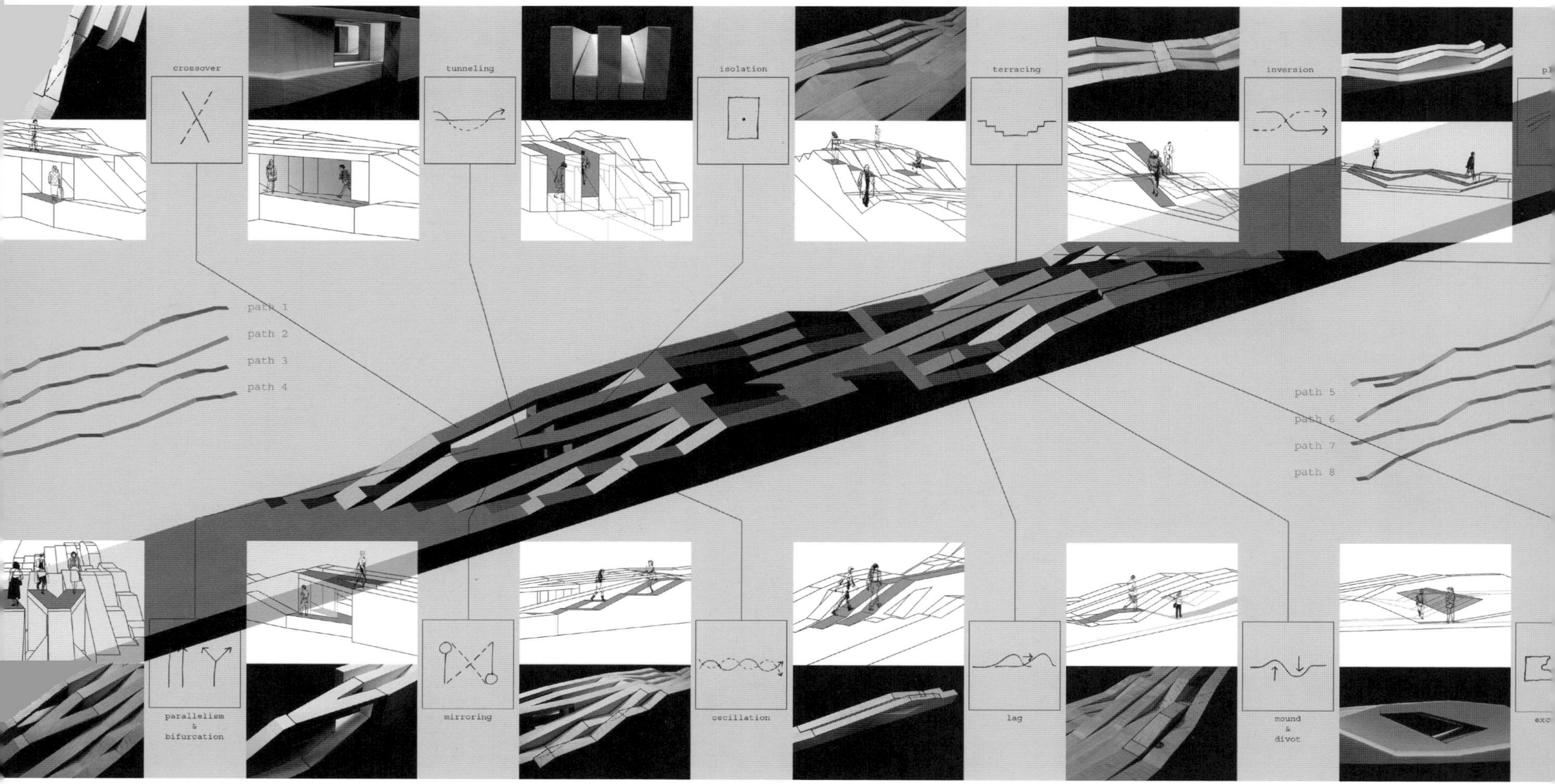
crossover
tunneling
isolation
terracing
inversion
path 1
path 2
path 3
path 4
path 5
path 6
path 7
path 8
parallelism & bifurcation
mirroring
oscillation
lag
mound & divot

actively renounce any striving for a nostalgia of the Home.

While this militant stance is not entirely unproblematic, those environments already compromised by a radical degree of non-dwelling—that is, (un)common spaces and times—provide a fertile ground for intervention through an architecture transformed from within by landscape. Could architecture potentially extract from these normally inert spaces certain figures of experience that might consist in creating, revealing, or simply allowing for singular moments to emerge from the flux of the mundane?

III.

One kind of space characterized more by its temporal dimension than its spatial attributes is the pedestrian tunnel. Such spaces, which serve only to link two separated things, have as their dominant attribute the experience of duration as one walks through them. One notable example is the tunnel in New York City connecting the Times Square subway station to the Port Authority bus terminal. While it separates two of the busiest hubs in Manhattan, it is a hermetically sealed tube with only two ways in and out, one at each end.

My investigation focused on that specific tunnel. In the first iteration of my intervention, the objective was to suggest that, during the time required to walk the tunnel, one could be traversing a much larger span of time by walking through topographies that have been shaped *by* time. To that end, the ancient and contemporary topographies that coincide with the site were compressed into the tunnel. **[Fig. 1]** The roofscape of the buildings currently adjoining the tunnel were logarithmically compressed into a series of planes and moved below to constitute the groundscape, whereas the pre-grid topography was extracted and extruded above to form an undulating roof membrane. Those two surfaces would then create a liminal zone through which the pedestrian would navigate while walking the length of the tunnel.

The problem with this conceptual move lay in the fact that it had nothing to do with how the individual actually moves within the space. Consequently, I shifted from the scale of the overall tunnel to moments in which movement could be articulated in ways that would counteract the homogenous linear dimension of the tunnel. This second phase **[Fig. 2]** was structured around the coordination of a singular encounter within the tunnel. Two people, approaching from opposite sides, would slip behind the walls and catch glimpses of each other at decreasing intervals through visual turrets before finally confronting each other across a gap lit by an oculus projecting light from above; all of the tectonic elements would conspire to create a moment of intensity centered around the gap. This encounter would take place against the backdrop of the mass flow of pedestrians, most of whom would pass under the bridge created by the encounter. In other words, this scheme staged the singular moment as being opposed to, or at least autonomous with respect to, the multitude.

The next iteration **[Fig. 3]** attempted to foster multiple transient relations between moving pedestrians. The tunnel was divided into eight parallel strips or striations, each three feet wide, a dimension chosen because it is comfortably occupied by one person while still allowing two people to pass each other, if necessary. Each striation combined with others at various points to form relations of movement; the resulting undulating ground plane became a catalog of tropes or configurations that could be formed by assemblages of striations. Although the endpoints of the undulations were determined subjectively, this process could logically be applied to the entire tunnel. The limits of this approach were, however, twofold: first, individual relations would be submerged and lost within the spectacle of the whole; second, the tunnel would risk the character of a theme park—however exciting the walk might be at first, it might soon become just as monotonous and irritating as an unvariegated tunnel.

The final phase of the investigation attempted to synthesize aspects of both the figural encounter and the multiple relations, so that the singular moment would remain distinct yet stand out from the field or ground due to a difference of degree rather than of kind.

The first proposed scheme **[Fig. 4]** was a reworking of the figural encounter, this time taking into account the flow of the whole. By convention, people in the United States tend to stay to the right when walking down corridors. If one were to place an obstacle in the path of that flow, certain general scenarios would emerge. A longitudinal element angled clockwise would reinforce the existing pattern of flow by channeling movement back towards the right edge on either side. An element angled counterclockwise, on the other hand, would disrupt the normal flow by diverting a portion towards the opposite edge, thereby creating occasions in which opposing flows would confront and merge into one another. Finally, an element placed at a specific height might be seen as an obstruction by some people but as something to be stepped onto or climbed over by others. In keeping with these speculations, the first intervention consists of a series of deflectors that operate on a gradient. These deflectors comprise a field of disturbances in the ground plane that gradually shift up and rotate counterclockwise. How each pedestrian navigates these deflectors will depend on the individual's perception; one can

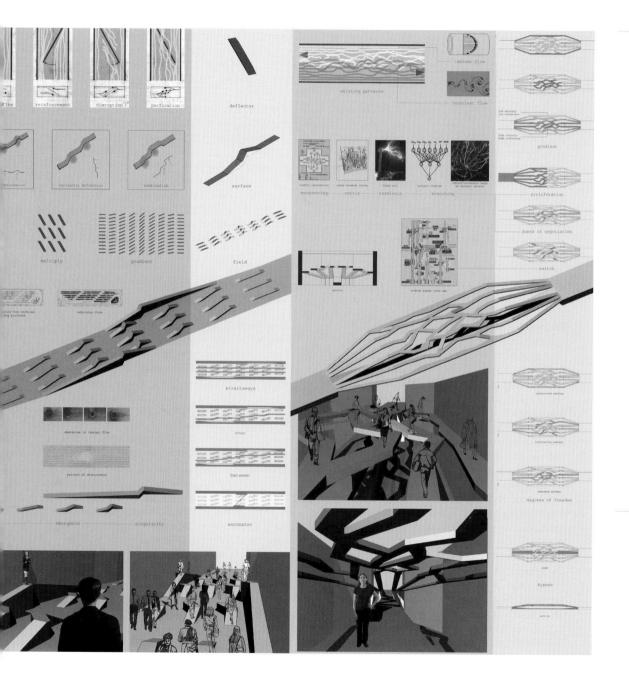

select a straightaway, walk over the deflectors, be channeled by the deflectors, or any combination of these three. Furthermore, the paths nearest the two walls gradually slope up in a protracted version of the smaller deflectors. These two paths reach the greatest height and are angled towards each other, allowing the people at the outer limits of the tunnel to glimpse each other before continuing on their way back down the path.

The second proposed scheme **[Fig. 5]** grew out of the crystallization of an existing pattern of movement within the tunnel. The smoothest but slowest movement (laminar flow) occurs near the walls; this is where those burdened with packages and suitcases, the elderly, and those simply not in a hurry tend to gravitate. The quickest but most agitated movement (turbulent flow) occurs near the middle of the tunnel, because those in a hurry will exploit the gap between the opposing flows to dodge and weave around the people in their way. The second intervention splits the tunnel into multiple paths that, from the edges to the center, gradually increase in both turbulence and degrees of freedom (i.e., the number of paths to which one can switch). As a foil, the scheme includes a bypass or path of withdrawal where one can slip underneath the mesh of pathways to observe the patterns of movement from below.

IV.

The anxiety of architecture today and its apparent disciplinary supercession by landscape stem from our fundamental, problematic relationship with the world of things. Living in a condition of radical non-dwelling, we are looking to the values of landscape to sustain architecture at a time when the severe clarity of the object is no longer seen as relevant. The complexity of the often invisible field, however, can defy comprehension by the subject of experience. It is here that architecture's ability to become a point of access to, connection with, and manipulation of various systems and forces that are always already around us can provide the means to new ways of living, thinking, and feeling. These projects are an attempt at revealing and influencing otherwise subconscious patterns of movement within a specific space, in order to allow for new moments of encounter with these systems and forces.

Acknowledgements: This project would not have been possible without the help of Phoebe Crisman, who taught the course on (un)common spaces; Sarah Drake, my research partner; and the thesis faculty (of which Ms. Crisman was a part): Jason Johnson (my advisor), Judy Kinnard, Beth Meyer, John Quale, Bill Sherman, and Peter Waldman.

Penley Chiang, M.Arch. (University of Virginia, 2003), is an architect currently working and non-dwelling in San Francisco. He can be contacted at penlex@yahoo.com.

Figures 4 & 5

NOTES

1 _ Gilles Deleuze, *Francis Bacon: The Logic of Sensation*, trans. Daniel W. Smith (Minneapolis: University of Minnesota Press, 2003), 52.
2 _ The thesis (2002-2003) was advised by Jason Johnson, and the seminar was taught by Phoebe Crisman.
3 _ Warner Bros., 1999.
4 _ Winy Maas, "Landscape," in *FARMAX* (Rotterdam: Uitgeverij 010, 1998), 96.
5 _ Martin Heidegger, "Building Dwelling Thinking," in *Poetry, Language, Thought*, trans. Albert Hofstadter (New York: Harper & Row, 1976), 159: "Usually we take production to be an activity whose performance has a result, the finished structure, as its consequence. It is possible to conceive of making in that way; we thereby grasp something that is correct, and yet never touch its nature, which is a producing that brings something forth...To the Greeks *techne* means neither art nor handicraft but rather: to make something appear, within what is present, as this or that, in this way or that way. The Greeks conceive of *techne*, producing, in terms of letting appear."
6 _ Massimo Cacciari, "Eupalinos or Architecture," trans. Stephen Sartarelli, in *Oppositions* 21 (Summer 1980): 395-397.
7 _ Ibid., 400.

Number of daily commuters through site

▭ = 50,000 people

Average commute time X Average commute speed = 46.8 miles

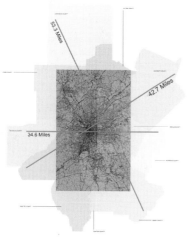

Metropolitan Atlanta

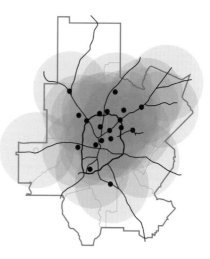

Average daily travel radius from activity centers

Average Atlanta Household 3.18

Average Atlanta Household 1.85

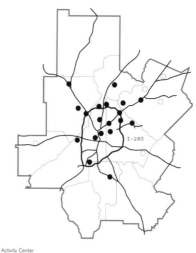

I-285

● Activity Center
○ Emerging Activity Center

The mapping of Atlanta's activity centers shows evidence of the higway's importance in the city to connect and disconnect the population across a large region

PUBLIC DOMAIN AND THE DISPERSED CITY

Hans Herrmann

As the automobile continues to gain influence over the planning and construction of cities, the charge of this thesis is to consider what may be gained from that development within the context of the dispersed city. Atlanta, Georgia, a city where the average citizen commutes more than two hours per day, is a condition comprising activity centers, shifting populations, and rapidly changing points of development. The system hinges on the automobile and its ability to bridge the supplies and demands that constitute Atlanta's critical mass. Highway infrastructure, forming the backbone of the city, demands more annual funding than nearly all other forms of civic development. Through that expense, the city demonstrates its mode and manner of engagement but little more. The highway's presence in Atlanta—as in many cities—is becoming greater in both its physical stature and its role as an agent of metropolitan life. Nevertheless, the benefits of the highway as public domain have been largely unexplored and unexploited. The opportunity to reinterpret and reconfigure the highway as public domain is available through the act of making tangible the civic and urban qualities already latent within the highway system. Through the framing and contextual manipulation of those qualities, form may be given to the changing physical and conceptual dimensions of contemporary public domain.

Plantings and growth

Park vegetation is carefully managed through intercropping, companion planting and a seasonal planting calendar. The Georgia Botanical garden is associated with the park, maintaining the flower mounds at the north west corner and the picnic areas in the northern end of the park. conifers and decidouus trees are grouped into clusters forming tight envelopes of forest space from which to experience the interchange both from the roadway and the pedestrian paths.

Hardscapes

The ground plane is surfaced with a varied field of materials to present opportunities for viewing and inhabiting the interchange at varying degrees of comfort. Each material is designed to allow for specific uses while permitting an open range of occupation. Where the roadway separates from the ground the delineation of volume is further articulated with curtaining devices that may be used for events of all sizes and type.

Wild Planting zones

The zones separated from the primary parcels by the highway are planted with wild flowers, grasses and trees requiring minimal maintenance and upkeep. The plantings provide an extension of the park to the highway surface while defining the pedestrian accessible bounds of the park.

The dispersed city—characterized by the rapid movement of information, people, and goods—is especially reliant upon systems of connective infrastructure. Within that dependence lies the potential to locate and activate an as yet undefined portion of the public domain. The systems of the dispersed city, being fluid and shifting rather than static and bundled, may be engaged only through a limited number of nodes. As a primary and physically tangible component of the dispersed city, the highway is an important area of exchange. The interchange, an exaggerated moment within the highway, is charged with overlaps and layerings of systems. Carefully designed and developed to accommodate the systems of the city, the space of the interchange offers a fixed point of engagement for this investigation.

Venue

Located at the intersection of Interstate 85 and Interstate 285 in northern Atlanta, the Moreland Interchange is a civic resource. Publicly constructed, owned, and operated, it presents itself as public domain through its support of public interests. The volume of traffic (over 300,000 passengers per day) and the highway's shared use by diverse—and even divergent—interests suggest the site's importance as a rich urban moment, albeit one where chance interaction is strictly limited by the bounds of the vehicle. The monumental size and scale of the space are also indicative of the city's chosen methods of development and inhabitation.

Monumentality is by definition suggestive of a public act or construct. Accordingly, the stature of the interchange should be filtered and manipulated by the elements of the design to heighten that sense of monumentality. Monumentality is not defined here in terms of commemoration or enshrinement: instead, the highway is a living monument constituted by the conditions of the city and its population. The strategy of this thesis is to provide new forms of access to the space of the interchange through the introduction and incorporation of an urban park. As a device, the park is designed to bring focus and articulation to the roadway's existing status as a public monument.

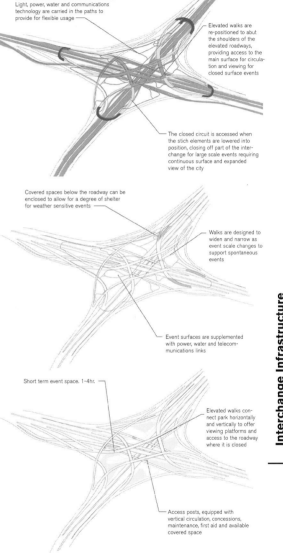

Paths line and cross the park based on border conditions between event surfaces. Light, power, water and communications technology are carried in the paths to provide for flexible usage

Elevated walks are re-positioned to abut the shoulders of the elevated roadways, providing access to the main surface for circulation and viewing for closed surface events

The closed circuit is accessed when the stich elements are lowered into position, closing off part of the interchange for large scale events requiring continuous surface and expanded view of the city

Covered spaces below the roadway can be enclosed to allow for a degree of shelter for weather sensitive events

Walks are designed to widen and narrow as event scale changes to support spontaneous events

Event surfaces are supplemented with power, water and telecommunications links

Short term event space. 1-4hr.

Elevated walks connect park horizontally and vertically to offer viewing platforms and access to the roadway where it is closed

Access posts, equipped with vertical circulation, concessions, maintenance, first aid and available covered space

Interchange Infrastructure

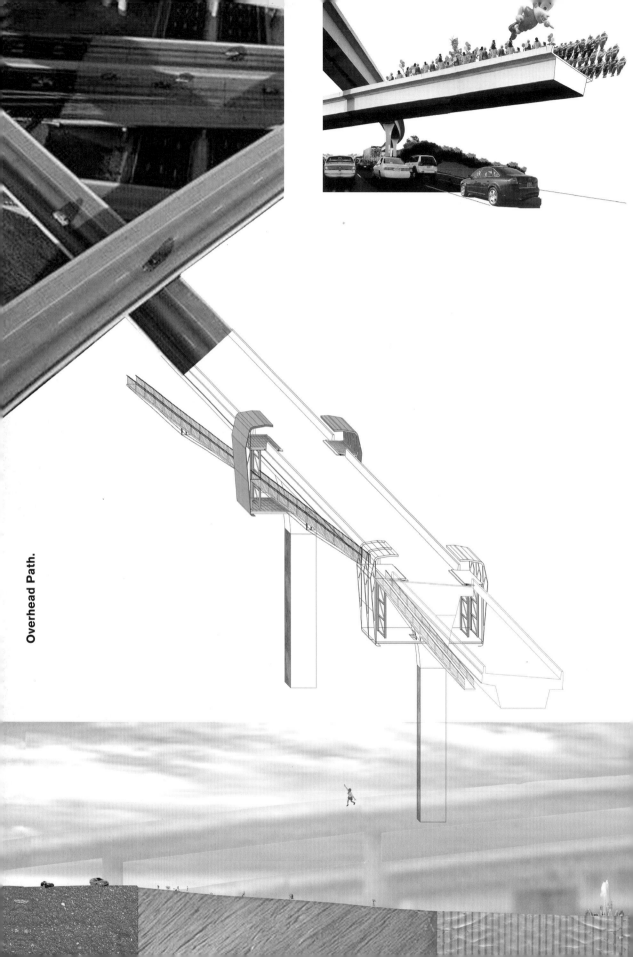

Overhead Path.

Access

The space of the interchange is to be supplemented with architectural and programmatic interventions working at the scale of the individual. Those elements and their associated uses begin to frame the space of the interchange both physically and socially, articulating the urbanity already present while adding secondary and tertiary layers of activation. Accessibility is vital, and takes on many forms, ranging from simple physical access, to the more abstract idea of a city-wide connection, to the interchange as a communal construct and identifiable destination. The park is thus conceived as a catalyst for exchange in its broadest sense.

Organizational Tactics

The park is arranged according to three structuring systems. One system is made up of a network of paths and event pads or surfaces that define activity zones both on and above the ground plane. The paths link event pads located throughout the park, while also carrying services that may be used to delineate individual event spaces. Power, water, and other utilities are supplemented by secondary sets of inlays (e.g., information-conveying conduits such as telephone lines, DSL, satellite feeds) that are accessed through the paths and pads. The pads and surfaces are paved, inlaid, or sometimes planted. To promote varying forms of occupation, the pads feature points of connection to the utilities supplied through the adjoining paths.

Throughout the course of a year, the paths and pads are opened and closed by a second structuring system: a carefully maintained program of plantings. The continual redefinition of space by shifting vegetation ensures a constant revitalization of the park as new venues and points of interest become available and familiar ones are closed off. In doing so, the park becomes a barometer of sorts through which the seasonal events and traditions of the city may be observed.

Given that the space of the interchange is largely conditioned by the daily cycle of traffic, time becomes the third structuring system. As conceived, the park has two temporal modes. The first is a twenty-four-hour park, comprised of the indeterminate spaces and events supported by the paths and pads, as well as the everyday points of operation such as service stations and welcome centers. The second mode is a carefully defined and choreographed set of events and venues that operate on a pre-determined timetable. That schedule is governed by a calendar of events decided upon by the city and its parks and recreation council. Those systems will function simultaneously to allow for overlaps of use and

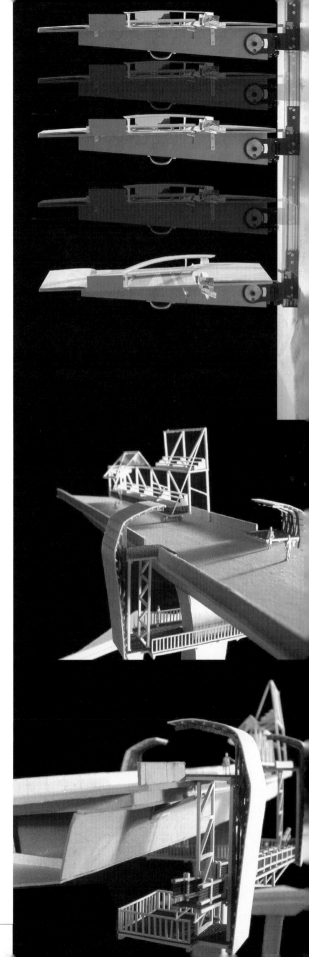

Jersey Barriers are modified and supplemented with electricity, water, and light to
provide for a wide range of use along the
perimeter path.

Paths are constructed from materials that allow for future
change. As the paths are occupied or ignored their place in
the landscape shifts. The pathways may then widen or narrow
based upon level of usage.

Directional louvers mounted on top of the
barriers are to be used in the manipulation
of sight lines, sound, light and wind. The
louvers can be changed depending on
space usage.

The ground is inlayed with various surfaces
which afford for multiple uses and are
contingent on weather, season, time of day,
activity duration and scale of event.

Frontage Zones.

occurrence to take place while within the space of the interchange and the city at large.

As a civic construct, the proposed park supplements the interchange by supplying it with new opportunities for access. Functioning in many different ways to serve the public, the park and interchange attempt to bring dialogue to, and between, the occupants of both spaces, while fostering a dynamic layering of activities and interactions.

Hans Curtis Herrmann, *M.Arch. (Clemson, 2003), currently lives and works in New York City. His personal work focuses on issues in urban development and on the relation of programmatic intent to material surface. At Clemson, he was awarded both the Saint Petersburg Prize for outstanding architectural design and the McClure Award, the top honor for graduate theses. His work has been exhibited nationally and internationally, most recently at "Beyond Media 2003: a Festival for Alternative Media in Architecture," sponsored by iMage in Florence, Italy.*

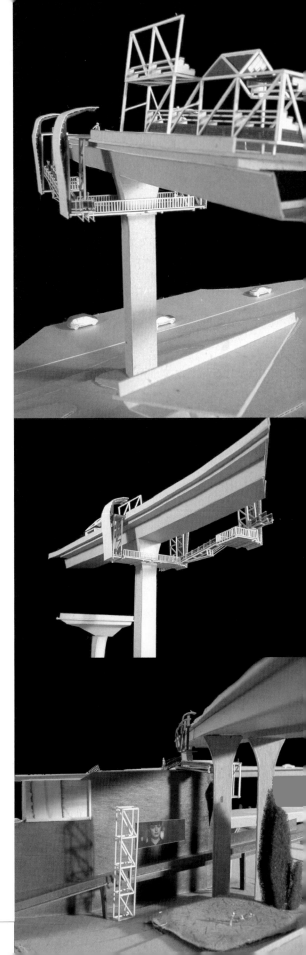

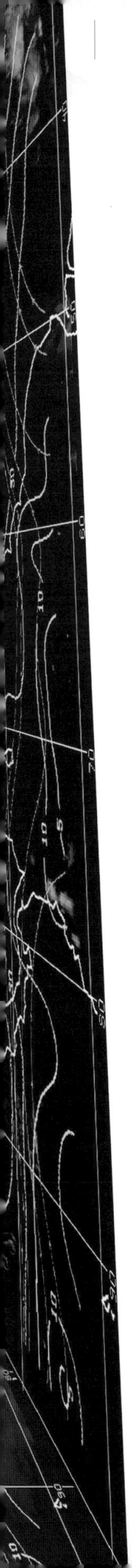

Hilary Sample

"AMBIENT ARCHITECTURE, AN ENVIRONMENTAL MONITORING STATION FOR PASADENA, CALIFORNIA

"*a metropolis that exists in a semi desert, imports water three hundred miles, has inveterate flash floods, is at the grinding edges of two tectonic plates, and has a microclimate tenacious of noxious oxides will have its priorities among the aspects that it attempts to control.*"

///// John McPhee, *The Control of Nature*

"*Ambient Music must be able to accommodate many levels of listening attention without enforcing one in particular; it must be as ignoble as it is interesting.*"

///// Brian Eno

This project investigates the idea of the ambient in architecture and envisions a seamless merger of architecture and environment. Architecture becomes a way to measure and register the environment; like a chameleon, architecture here becomes background. Ambient architecture is where the distinction between nature and architecture is blurred. Like the weather, which is always in a state of change, ambient architecture is predicated on a responsive relationship.

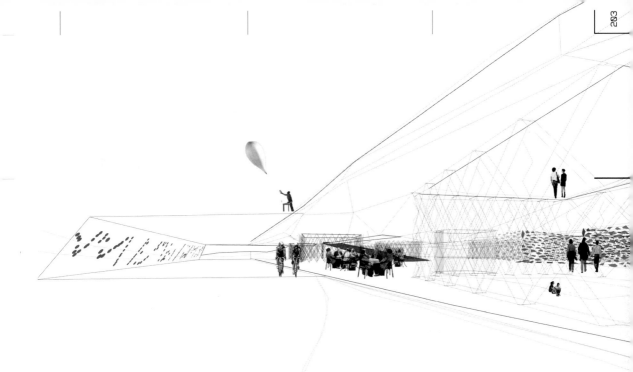

In ambient architecture, oppositions such as public and private, interior and exterior, and landscape and building become irrelevant, primarily because those notions rely upon determined fixities of image, form, and program that are excluded here. Bruno Latour describes that paradigm in his book *Science and Action* (1987), which focuses attention on scientific principles of "mobility, combinability and stability."[1] Latour's understanding of mobility and combinability influenced this thesis through the idea of architecture as a system responsive to the environment. Stability, seemingly inevitable in architecture, is here an attempt to create a stable sense of instability through the incorporation of technologies that react to the changing environment, like sensing devices. Specific technologies yet to be developed are imagined as design elements to be exploited in an investigation focusing on their application throughout the building, with an emphasis on façades as sensing devices. Conceived in that way, façades register temperature, humidity, precipitation, and pollutants, thereby altering their reading. In this instance, the façade is both stabile as a system and unstable as an iteration. In ambient architecture, forms and spaces shift in and out of focus and fixity is suppressed in favor of instability and new potentials, following the paradigm of weather. Ambient architecture performs through a continuous scoring, notating and

transforming of its shifting climatic, programmatic, and geological conditions.

These ideas are pursued through a proposal for an environmental or ambient monitoring station (AMS), to be situated within an environmental landmark—the Hahmongha Park and Arroyo Seco—along the Foothills Freeway in Pasadena, California. The AMS is a research facility and public education center focused on ambient air quality and its relationship to weather. Whereas institutions such as the Green Building at MIT, National Oceanic and Atmospheric Administration (NOAA), and the National Center for Atmospheric Research (NCAR) limit interaction between researchers and exclude public interest, the AMS incorporates facilities for both research and public engagement, including an archive, gallery, and spaces for presentation to the public. Furthermore, the AMS introduces a dispersed and linear form in which, for example, an entrance for researchers coincides with a cafeteria for visitors in an attempt to stimulate exchange among all users.

The AMS is in close proximity to institutions, such as schools, other research institutions, park services, and emergency services. It operates within an urban context and draws on the scientific communities of Los Angeles and Pasadena, including the California Institute of Technology and NASA's Jet Propulsion Laboratory (JPL). Based

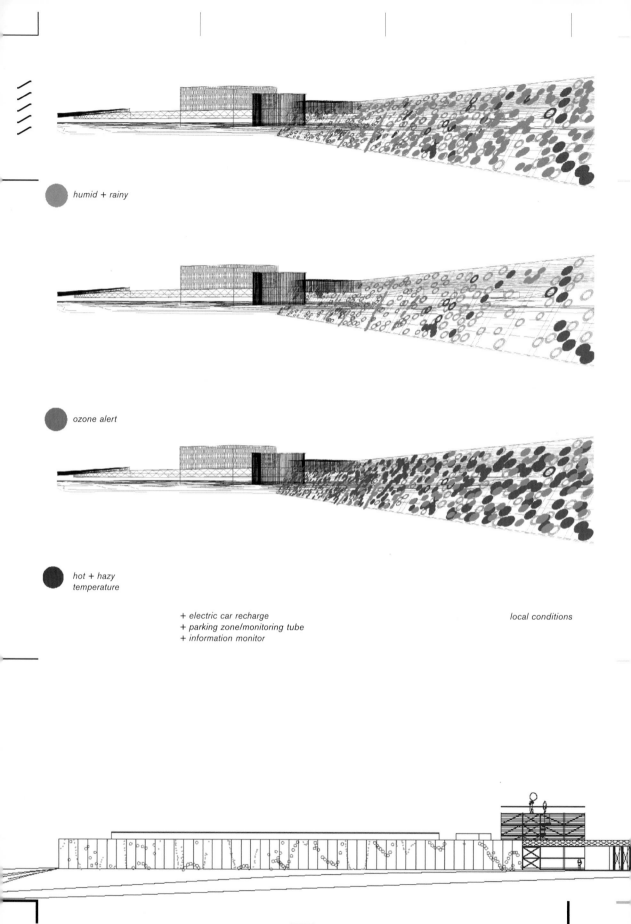

humid + rainy

ozone alert

hot + hazy
temperature

+ electric car recharge
+ parking zone/monitoring tube
+ information monitor

local conditions

loosely on a new program being developed by the Environmental Protection Agency,[2] the AMS includes components of hard science such as laboratories, sensing devices, and archives and introduces a softer idea of public components such as exhibition spaces, a lecture hall, an open archive, and simulation rooms. The public components draw inspiration from the Griffith Observatory roof top observation deck and the ability to rent telescopes remotely for a few hours in the evening at the nearby Mt. Wilson Observatory.

A unifying ground of landscape flows throughout the AMS, maintaining a constant state of instability as the architecture dissolves into the environment. This proposal seeks to engage a public program with a scientific research institution while mediating between people, scientific data as digital information, and the atmosphere. This project investigates the limits of nature and culture and calls into question their opposition. Limits are explored through site and environmental sensors that include a wide variety of devices

designed to measure, test, and signal changes in environmental conditions, including visible/invisible wavelength, temperature, moisture and dew point, smoke, dust and opacity, light, and weather. The AMS addresses possible new organizations for the exchange of information through a distributed network that operates performatively, rethinking the institutional form through the concept of the field, the environment, society, and the landscape. The AMS is a communicative architecture that remains incomplete, subject to the free flow of information and exchange resulting from its environment.

Simulation rooms located on level with the park juxtapose natural aspects of the local environment with the potentials of the global environment, imported via technology and scientific networks. The flexibility of these simulation rooms allows for multi- and interdisciplinary exploration, accommodating a scientist and intern observing a weather event as readily as presentations to the public. Combining digital information from the local field as well as from satellites, environmental

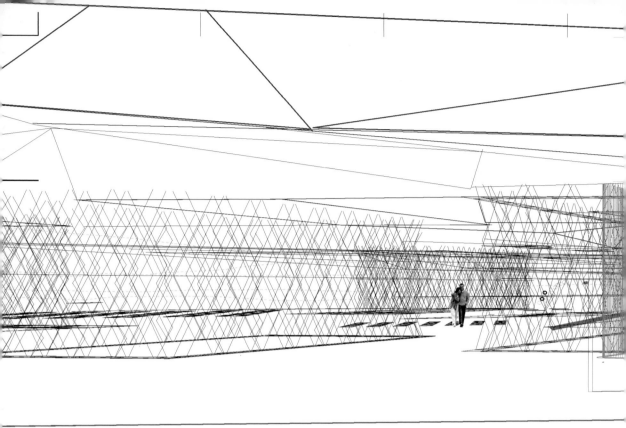

information is accessible in new forms; here, architecture is part of the interface between people and information. At the AMS, vegetation blends into the architecture with help from indigenous oxygen regeneration plantings. The planted field condition reacts to the environment, acting as a biological sensor and displaying positive or negative effects of its surroundings. An area planted with yellow specimens remains yellow in good conditions but turns brown where it has been adversely affected by the environment. These planted areas are the largest sensing devices in the AMS.

As part of a park system, bike and walking paths circulate throughout the AMS. The roof is both an extended ground plane of the park and an environmental system that keeps research and public spaces temperate. Devices for monitoring the microclimatic conditions of southern California are dispersed throughout the AMS. Balloon launching platforms, along with wind recording devices, air filters, and a roof top observation deck, complete the system of elements engaging the landscape.

Ambient Monitoring Station

Level +1—At this level, the AMS is organized by infrastructure, collection, and dispersal. The landscape infrastructure ties into the existing Hahmongha Park system while concurrently providing the structural and technical infrastructure for the ambient monitoring station. The building's primary structural system is a pneumatic truss, which allows for the ceiling to expand and contract as necessary to service the variable programmatic spaces below. Placing all of the services (mechanical, electrical, storage, and data distribution) within the ceiling frees up the floor plane, allowing mobility, combinability, and stability—the principles outlined by Latour in *Science and Action*.

Level 0—Interpretation and interface are the primary functions of this level. As the main level of the AMS, it mixes public and research facilities, focusing on the paradigm of combinability. Activities at the AMS consist of exhibitions, archiving of weather information, browsing computing labs, educational demonstrations, and engagement with local and global environments. The pneumatic truss system helps provide mobility and programmatic flexibility.

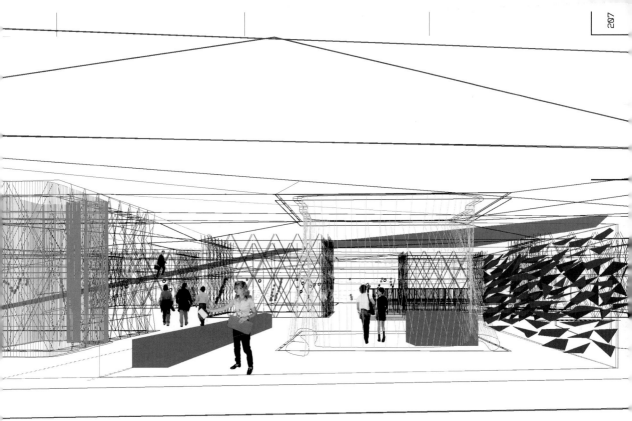

Level -1—Simulation, expansion, and research are the structuring concerns of this level, which engages the ground plane of the Oak Grove Park. The AMS operates here as a research filter, consolidating data into a series of simulation rooms that in turn provide an immersive digital environment of information and simulation. Each of these rooms provides a unique micro-environment according to the research. Architecturally, these rooms are perhaps the most stable in a conventional sense, although accommodating the sublime experience of real-time research.

Hilary Sample, *M.Arch. (Princeton, 2003), is an Assistant Professor in the Faculty of Architecture, Landscape, and Design at the University of Toronto. She is also the recipient of the 2004-05 Reyner Banham teaching Fellowship at the University of Buffalo. As an architect, her work focuses on the intersection between architecture, technology, and the environment. Developed as an M.Arch. thesis project under the direction of Stan Allen,* Ambient Architecture *was awarded the Suzanne Kolarik Underwood Prize at Princeton and was presented at the Eco Wave Conference, San Francisco, in 2003.*

NOTES

1_ Bruno Latour, *Science in Action* (Cambridge, MA: Harvard University Press, 1987), 223.
2 _ Concerning the EPA's new ambient monitoring information program, see http://www.epa.gov/ttn/amtic/

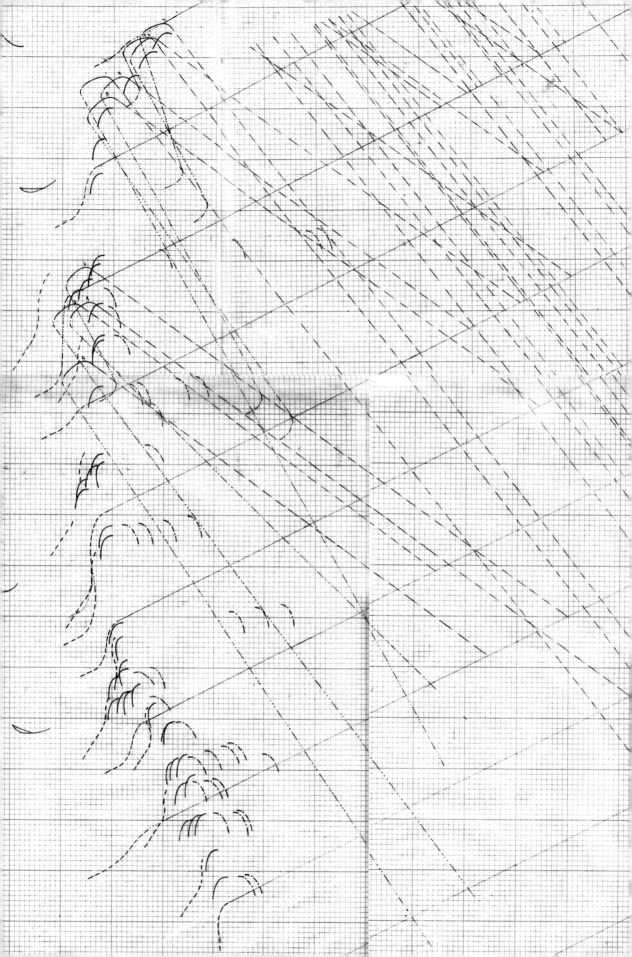